DIY EMF Home Inspection Guide

Learn How to Eliminate Harmful Radiation from Your Home

Brian R. Humrich, Ph.D.

ISBN: 9798581466025

This book contains advice and information relating to health care. It is not intended to replace medical advice and it is recommended that you seek your physician's advice prior to starting any medical program or treatment. The author disclaims liability for any medical outcomes that may occur as a result of applying the methods suggested in this book.

Book design by Brian Humrich.
Photos by Max Tuta Noronha

First printing edition 2020.

www.EHSwarrior.com

To all of those who wish to
live a healthier lifestyle

TABLE OF CONTENTS

Preface

~

When I first started learning about the associated risks wireless radiation posed to health, the information on the subject wasn't readily available. Not to mention the information that did exist was written by professionals for professionals. This made understanding the dangers difficult for the lay person. I remember reading article after article on a website called "PubMed" about complex subjects like "EMFs and there effect on VGCCs", and "EMFs and Apoptosis."

Fast forward a few years and the information that was once difficult to obtain and comprehend, exploded into a plethora of easily understood books that were available anywhere books were sold. With a new book on the subject of wireless radiation or EMFs coming out almost monthly, I purchased each and every one of them, consuming their words in a single reading session and then eagerly awaiting the next author to publish his or her findings. However, after about the twentieth book read, I began noticing a trend in the text. Each author discussed the science behind how wireless radiation and EMFs were negatively impacting our health, some discussed ways in which you can reduce your exposure and only one discussed detection techniques. It seemed that each author was writing about the same things, with little to no actionable steps that could be taken to make your environment radiation free.

For me, living in an environment free of wireless radiation was necessary due to health complications so figuring out how to create that environment was of the utmost importance. I spent years learning the ins and outs of wireless radiation and EMFs and eventually perfected the process of creating an environment that was radiation free. I even got to the point where I developed a product that measures the amount of electricity within the body at any given time (patent pending).

After curing myself of all my health complications, I became even more obsessed with the positive impact living in an environment free of wireless radiation had and started helping others mimic my lifestyle. What started out as an attempt to replicate my positive results eventually grew into a business due to its extreme success. In fact, the results of my first few clients were so positive that people from other states and even other countries started reaching out to me, asking if I could come inspect their homes for radiation. Week after week my schedule increased, all without advertising. I even worked with a doctor who made it mandatory for her patients to get an EMF home inspection if they wanted to work with her. All because she was a firm believer that health is affected by both internal and external forces. Eventually I had far too many clients for one person to keep up with and decided there had to be a better way to help more people. That is where the idea for this guide originated.

I originally created this guide in an attempt to reach the people that needed my help that were too far away for me to travel to. Inadvertently, it turned into much more than that. Clients of mine began asking for copies so that they could continue doing their own inspections, people with EHS (electromagnetic hypersensitivity) started asking for copies to help better explain to their family members how wireless radiation is a problem that can be easily fixed, and doctors began asking for copies to hand out to their patients who could benefit from a less radiation filled environment. One doctor even started calling it a way to "disconnect to reconnect." I couldn't have even begun to imagine just how popular this guide became and yet at the same time it made perfect sense. People care about their health and when you find something that works you tell everyone you know, and then they tell everyone they know and so on. It's contagious. Chances are if you are reading this then you are interested in inspecting your own home for wireless radiation and EMFs. You care about your health and want to learn how to create an environment that is radiation free. This guide will help you take control of the EMF radiation in your life and feel the difference immediately by learning how to detect and mitigate high sources of radiation from: radio frequencies, electric fields, magnetic fields and dirty electricity. I am glad this guide reached your hands.

Introduction

~

One of my favorite quotes of all times is "knowledge is power", and after discovering just how different I was in an EMF free environment, I felt powerful. It was as if I had been living in black and white my entire life and someone flipped on the color. Discovering that man made EMFs are actually harmful changed my life.

I know what you are thinking, "what are EMFs?" Simply put, EMFs or Electromagnetic Frequencies are a form of radiation comprised of four categories:

1. Electric Fields
2. Magnetic Fields
3. Radio Frequencies
4. Dirty Electricity

Throughout this guide we will dive deeper into each category, explaining what each one is, where they can be found, and ways to reduce them. You will also learn how to properly assess and perform your own home inspection for EMF radiation as well as a step by step guide on proper remediation techniques.

Below I have broken down some of the more frequently asked questions regarding the subject of EMF home inspections. It is my goal to make this guide as easy to follow as possible so that the average person with zero experience with EMFs can conduct their own inspection as comfortably and accurately as possible. If at any point you are confused or need further assistance, I have included a section at the end of this guide with links, books and various other helpful references.

What is an EMF home inspection?

An EMF home inspection is an inspection of a home's radio frequency radiation, magnetic field, electric field, and dirty electricity. Otherwise known as EMF level inspections within a home. In today's homes the levels of EMF radiation have reached severely unsafe heights, resulting in an abundance of health-related symptoms. By inspecting one's home for EMF levels, you may find that the environment is less than satisfactory, resulting in the need for remediation.

Why are EMF home inspections important?

An EMF home inspection is necessary for anyone who cares about the health and safety of themselves or their family. Today we live in a world where the devices we rely so heavily on and that have become such an integral part of our lives have not been adequately tested for safety. If you remember back to when cigarettes were once said to be safe, you'll understand where we are at today with certain technologies. EMFs are the new cigarettes, and we are addicted now more than ever. By conducting an EMF home inspection, you will learn just how saturated your life is with technology and that without certain devices you will actually sleep better, heal faster, and live happier lives.

Who can conduct an EMF home inspection?

There are numerous professional companies that will come out to your home and conduct an EMF home inspection for you, but that can be pricey. After reading this guide you will have a very good understanding of how to conduct your own home inspection and can invest the money you would have spent on your very own professional meters. When I first learned about all the dangers of EMFs, I started out by conducting home inspections on my home as well as my friends and family's homes. The little changes that I made as well as the inspections themselves saved them thousands of dollars and provided me with more experience. After seeing a noticeable improvement in all of their health, I knew I was on to something and began conducting EMF home inspections for anyone and everyone interested. Anyone with the correct meters and the knowledge gained from this guide can start doing their own EMF home inspections immediately.

How long does an inspection take?

There are various factors to take into consideration when determining the time it may take to complete an inspection. For example, a typical inspection lasts anywhere from 1-5 hours but I have had some span over numerous days adding up to well over 16 hours. Some of my clients are extremely knowledgeable about EMFs and complete as much as possible on their own and then call me in to check their work and make any revisions they may have missed. Those inspections last approximately an hour. Then there are clients of mine that know absolutely nothing about EMFs and those appointments take approximately 4-5 hours. Also, the size of the home and the number of occupants are additional factors to take into consideration. Larger homes take more time to walk around with your meters, and more occupants means more time spent explaining the dangers of their individual devices. Also, in order to cover all of the categories of EMFs, you will be conducting multiple different inspections — such as a radio frequency inspection, magnetic field inspection, electrical field inspection, and a dirty electricity inspection. To be safe I always recommend to the client that they have at least 8 hours of free time before scheduling a home inspection. It's better to have more time than less.

When should an inspection be performed?

Most of the clients that I conduct home inspections for are due to existing health reasons but my recommendation is to perform one prior to getting to that point. In a perfect world I would conduct an inspection prior to moving into a new home. That way a baseline is gathered of the space before any potentially harmful devices are brought into the home. However, that may not be possible and you may already live in the home you wish to inspect. In that case, I would perform one right away.

How much does an EMF home inspection cost?

A typical EMF home inspection can range anywhere from $500-$5,000 depending on the professional company that you hire. However, that is only for the inspection itself and does not include the price of the remediation. After reading this guide you will be able to conduct your own EMF home inspection and complete the remediation process yourself, saving yourself thousands of dollars. The only investment you will have to make is in the meters used to detect EMFs, which will be covered thoroughly in the meters chapter.

Getting Started

~

Prior to conducting an EMF home inspection, understanding what you will be doing is critical. Although this chapter may seem redundant, it is important to understand what you are going to be doing during an EMF home inspection prior to investing your time and money. Below I have broken down the steps you will be taking during an inspection in an easy to follow format. Then in the following chapters you will learn each step individually in order to further understand the ins and outs of what goes into inspecting and remediating a home of EMF radiation.

Step 1- Purchase necessary EMF detecting meters.

Step 2- Fill out necessary pre inspection checklist, and look up your home or space you are inspecting on the website antennasearch.com.

Step 3- Conduct baseline measurement of exterior and

interior of home or space you are inspecting prior to starting the actual inspection.

Step 4- Conduct **exterior** inspection with radio frequency meter and remediate if necessary.

Step 5- Conduct **interior** inspection with radio frequency meter and remediate if necessary.

Step 6- Conduct **exterior** inspection with magnetic field meter and remediate if necessary.

Step 7- Conduct **interior** inspection with magnetic field meter and remediate if necessary.

Step 8- Conduct **exterior** inspection with electric field meter and body voltage meter and remediate if necessary.

Step 9- Conduct **interior** inspection electric field meter and body voltage meter and remediate if necessary.

Step 10- Conduct **exterior** inspection with dirty electricity meter (if home has exterior outlets) and remediate if necessary.

Step 11- Conduct **interior** inspection with dirty electricity meter and remediate if necessary.

Step 12- Make sure documentation is provided with baseline measurements as well as after remediation measurements.

Step 13- Set up a future date to conduct a reinspection

of the above steps again. This can be done weekly, monthly or annually depending on your individual needs.

Throughout this guide you will learn each of the steps necessary to conducting an EMF home inspection. Above is merely a compiled list of the steps for your reference. Until you are familiar with the steps, I advise you to keep a copy at your disposal as a quick reference guide.

Step 1-

EMF Meters

The absolute most important aspect of completing and EMF home inspection is the meters that you use. Without quality meters you won't gain an accurate measurement which could ruin the entire inspection. For example, when I first started out learning the dangers of EMFs, I purchased a TriField 2 EMF meter. At the time it was what I could afford and honestly, I had no clue about how ineffective it was at detecting EMFs. I went around my parent's entire house, switching from magnetic field to electric field and to radio frequencies trying to find the "problem areas" without any real idea what I was looking for. Unfortunately, the meter came with zero instructions on what to look for, what the numbers on the screen meant, or what safe levels were considered once I did find what I was looking for. So, I spent hours searching with the meter in my hand hoping that the answers would light up on the screen, but they didn't. Instead the only thing I came up with was that I was unsure whether or not the house was good or bad.

Not having a quality meter led me to believe that my parent's house wasn't as bad as it actually was. That was a mistake I never made again.

For several years I went through various meters trying to figure out which ones were the best at detecting the problem. I would purchase a meter, try it out, learn that the descriptions didn't match the product, and return it. Eventually I found the absolute perfect meters for detecting all of the different categories of EMFs and have listed them below. I know that they may seem a little expensive and therefore I have categorized them in a way to reflect which ones should be purchased first. However, if you are looking to get a true understanding of how good or bad your home is then purchasing the meters below is necessary. There are numerous meters on the market that claim that they can accomplish the same thing as the meters I have listed below, but after trying them myself I can assure you that they don't even come close. Worst case scenario you can do what I did and buy them, try them yourself, and return them once you discover that they don't work to the level in which they claim. Make sure to check the return policy though if that is something you are going to do. I wouldn't want you to purchase a meter that has a no return policy.

One of the meters listed below is one in which I invented, called *The Body Voltage Meter*, patent pending. Due to the status of the world today (COVID-19), I am still waiting on a manufacturer to purchase the design and begin producing it. This works out well for you, because I am going to include how to build your own using a multimeter.

Below I have broken down each meter into specific categories in order to further explain what each one does as well as the recommended safe levels associated with exposures related to that specific field measurement.

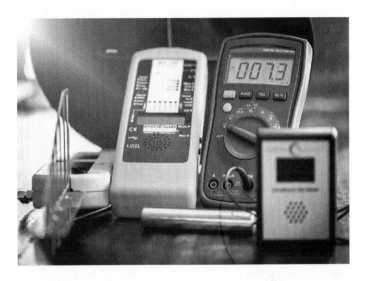

Meter #1
Name: HF-35C
Cost: $400.00
Measures: Radio Frequencies
Range: 800 MHz-2.5 GHz

This is the meter that I use the absolute most and would not trade in for any other. With this device you are only able to measure radio frequencies (I cannot stress that enough). Some individuals may think that it measures magnetic fields, electric fields, and dirty electricity, but it does not. Each meter measures different types of EMFs, and this one measures radio frequencies. This is the meter that you will use during your radio frequency inspection and remediation. It is available on Amazon and LessEMF.com.

Using this meter is simple. There are three main buttons that you need to worry about:

1. On/Off
2. Peak/RMS
3. 1-199.9 $\mu W/m^2$ / 200-1,999 $\mu W/m^2$

There isn't an explanation needed for the On/Off button, just know that in order to use the meter it needs to be in the "On" position. Once the device is on, you will then have to decide between using the "Peak" or "RMS" option. The peak option is what I recommend keeping the meter on. What this means is that it will measure the highest level of radio frequencies or the "peak" of the wave. The RMS option measures the average of the readings. After selecting the peak option then you will have to select between two different ranges of measuring capabilities. However, it is always a good idea to start with the lower range first (1-199.9 $\mu W/m^2$). If you are taking measurements and the levels exceed 199.9 $\mu W/m^2$, a 1--- will show up on the screen. By switching to the higher range (200-1,999 $\mu W/m^2$) you will then be able to read the radio frequency level if it does not exceed 1,999 $\mu W/m^2$. If it does then a 1--- will show up on the screen as well. You may be thinking: what do these numbers mean? Before explaining what these numbers mean, let me first describe what this meter measures. This meter measures radio frequency devices, which means anything that sends a wireless signal. For example:

1. Cell phones
2. DECT landline phones
3. Anything Bluetooth
4. Smart devices and appliances
5. Cell towers (3G,4G,5G, etc.)
6. WiFi

The list above is merely an example of the different radio frequency emitting devices. All of which can be measured using the HF-35C radio frequency meter.

Each of these devices emits different levels of pulsed radio frequencies, measured in units called micro watts or μW. The m² stands for meter squared. Put that all together and you have microwatts per meter squared or $\mu W/m^2$. Although the recommended safe levels are technically below .1 $\mu W/m^2$, below I have broken down the difference between no problem at all (safe) and an extreme problem (unsafe):

<.1 = No problem
.1-10 = Slight problem
10-1000 = Severe problem
>1000 = Extreme problem

When using the meter, all that you do is point the antenna at the device that you want to measure and it will show up on the screen. Then depending on which category it falls under, you can determine if that device is safe or unsafe to use. Another feature of the HF-35C is that it has an audible function. Near the top of the meter is a sound knob that allows you to adjust the sound levels. Once it is adjusted, point the meter at a device that gives off radio frequency radiation (cell phone, WiFi, Bluetooth, etc.) and listen to what that specific radiation sounds like. Being that wireless radio frequency radiation is invisible, the audio function makes it visible. You will soon see that every device makes a different sound and all of them sound very intimidating, so if you are in public you may want to keep the volume lower. If you are curious as to what a certain sound coming off of your meter is, there are websites that actually have various radio frequency sounds and will let you know what you are measuring. If you are measuring something with long increments of pulsed signals like a smart meter, make sure to wait at least a minute while pointing the meter in its direction. Sometimes, certain devices will show a zero reading on the meter and then a minute later it will pulse levels much higher. Another example of this is accomplished by placing your phone on the table in front of you and waiting for a text message to come through while the meter is pointed at it. When a text message (or call) comes through, the meter will spike and then drop back down to a lower level.

When measuring radio frequencies using this radio frequency meter, it is always a good idea to gain 3 different measurements at varying distances, such as:

1. 1" away
2. 12" or 1' away
3. 36" or 3' away

By doing so you are able to determine safe or unsafe distances for the various radio frequency radiation emitting devices in your life. For example: most people use their cell phones pressed up against their ears. Therefore, when testing the radio frequency levels, it is a good idea to test it with the antenna of the meter on the phone. That way, you are able to determine the amount of radiation you are being exposed to with a cell phone up against your head.

Without this meter, you won't be able to measure radio frequency radiation levels properly. If you are interested in purchasing a more advanced meter, don't. There are a few other models that are similar to the HF-35C that are capable of measuring a wider spectrum of frequencies but as you just learned, if its above .1 $\mu W/m^2$ then it is unsafe. In other words, you don't need to be able to read how high it is as long as you know it's unsafe. If you are going to be doing home inspections as a business however, purchasing a meter more advanced than the HF-35C may be necessary, especially with measuring 5G levels. For more advanced meters, stick to the same family as the HF-35C meter and look for the meters associated with Gigahertz Solutions.

Meter #2
Name: The Body Voltage Meter
Cost: $100.00
Measures: Body voltage from A/C electric fields
Range: Will vary depending on multimeter used

Besides the HF-35C radio frequency meter, having a body voltage meter is a must have. Although this was a device that I invented and have a patent pending on, I am going to show you how to make your own using a multimeter. Prior to showing you how, first let me explain the importance of this meter by asking you a simple question: do you know your body voltage where you are sitting right now? If you answered no, then you are like the majority of the clients I have done home inspections for. What body voltage is measuring, is the amount of electricity currently flowing through your body. You essentially want zero electricity flowing through your body, but in most homes that is not the case. Just to give you an idea, electricity is measured in volts. Anything below .1 volts (V) or 100 millivolts (mV) is considered safe. In the average bed, the body voltage while sleeping is around 2.5 volts or 2,500 mV. That means that you have 2.5 volts of electricity flowing through your body while you sleep. By lowering your body voltage to below .1 volts or 100 mV, your body will have an opportunity to reach new levels of health. For more information on this, see the electric field inspection and remediation chapter. On the next page you will learn how to make your own body voltage meter, so that you too can know how much electricity is flowing through your body at any given point during the day or night.

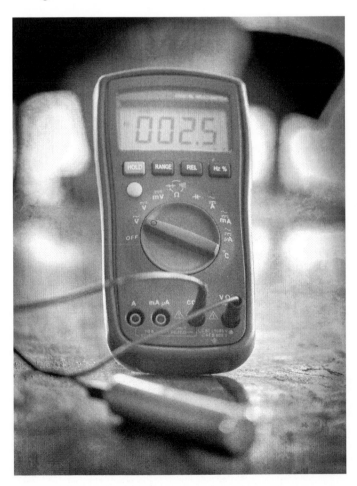

1. Purchase a digital multimeter that is capable of measuring in millivolts. On average, one that is under $40.00 will work just fine.

2. Purchase a grounding cable that is capable of being plugged into the wall as well as capable of plugging into the multimeter. The ones that are available should have a removable alligator clip. Under that clip is the portion that you will be plugging into the multimeter. These are typically $20.00 on Amazon.

3. When the multimeter arrives, plug the grounding cable into the port that is labeled "com".

4. Then plug the other end of the grounding cable into the ground portion of a wall outlet.

5. Next plug the red cable that comes with the multimeter into the red port that is labeled (V) for Volts.

6. Then turn the dial on the multimeter to measure A/C Volts. On most multimeters it will look like a V with a ~ on top of it.

7. Once it is on, hold the metal portion of the red cable in between your fingers. In the picture on the previous page you will notice a silver handle. That is because I made a handle that the red cable inserts into, expanding on the metal piece.

8. If you want to make a handle, find anything that is metal (an old drawer handle works) and clamp the alligator clip to it. Then hold the handle in your hand.

9. Now hold the metal end of the red cable in one hand, and the multimeter in the other and lay down in your bed (make sure it is also

plugged into the ground portion of your outlet). The number that pops up on your multimeter is the amount of electricity flowing through your body. Remember, higher than .1 Volts or 100mV is considered unsafe.

Meter #3
Name: Green Wave Dirty Electricity Meter
Cost: $150.00
Measures: Dirty electricity from electromagnetic interference on powerlines.
Range: 0 mV-1,999 mV

The Green Wave dirty electricity meter makes measuring dirty electricity as simple as plugging the meter into a wall outlet. Once the meter is plugged into the wall, it measures the amount of dirty electricity present in that specific circuit. According to the manufacturers of this meter, a measurement of below 25 millivolts (mV) is recommended. This meter, along with the 2 others previously listed are the top 3 meters that I would purchase if looking to start inspecting your home of EMFs.

The Green Wave meter will only measure the amount of dirty electricity present within the home. It does not measure any of the other categories of EMFs. There is one other dirty electricity meter on the market that I am familiar with called the Graham-Stetzer meter. Unfortunately, it measures in GS units (named after their names) and is a little more expensive than the Green Wave meter. If you come across this meter, feel free to try it out as well. Both of them work very similarly and have money back guarantees listed on their websites.

Meter #4
Name: NFA 1000
Cost: $2,100.00
Measures: Electric and Magnetic Fields
Range: 5 Hz – 1,000,000 Hz

I am choosing to recommend this meter last solely because of its price. The NFA 1000, although very pricey, is by far the best meter that I own. Compared to the many electric and magnetic field meters that I have tested, this one stands out like a sore thumb. Like the HF-35C it was made my Gigahertz Solutions in Germany. It measures electric fields and magnetic fields only but does so with amazing precision. Located on the device are numerous buttons, all of which have a specific function. The NFA 1000 is black and comes wrapped in a yellow rubber protective case. No antenna is provided with this meter, instead it uses an internal based antenna. However, an exterior antenna can be purchased for around $250.00 and is called a "TC03". This antenna looks like a large green plate, approximately 12" in diameter and enhances the overall measuring capabilities.

Using the NFA 1000 is very simple once you get the hang of it. For magnetic field measurements make sure that the button labeled "M3D" is selected. M3D stands for magnetic field 3 dimensional. What that means is that it will measure the magnetic field on a 3-dimensional axis. See below for what that looks like:

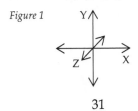

Figure 1

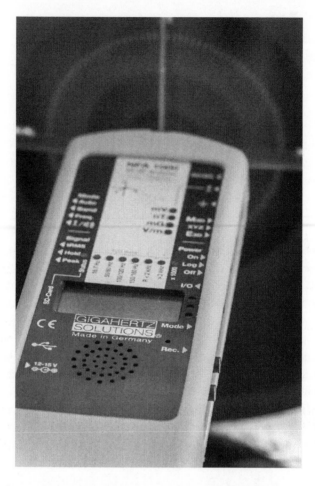

When measuring the magnetic field, all that you need to do is point the meter at the device in question and if a magnetic field is present, it will be reflected in a number on the meter. Magnetic field is measured in both milligauss (mG) and nanotesla (nT) on the meter. The magnetic field recommended levels are listed on the following page.

<20 = No problem
20-100 = Slight problem
100-500 = Severe problem
>500 = Extreme problem

When measuring magnetic fields using the NFA 1000, it is always a good idea to gain 3 different measurements at varying distances, such as:

1. 1" away
2. 12" or 1' away
3. 36" or 3' away

By doing so you are able to determine safe or unsafe distances for the various magnetic field emitting devices in your life. For example: one device that emits high levels of magnetic fields is a blow dryer. Chances are, if you own a blow dryer you use it a few inches from your head. So, when measuring the magnetic field of a blow dryer, place the meter the same distance away that you would have it while using it on your head. That way you are able to gain an accurate measurement of how much of a magnetic field you are exposing your brain to on a daily basis. For other magnetic field examples, see the magnetic field chapter on inspecting and remediation.

Along with magnetic fields, this meter also measures electric fields. In order to measure electric fields, switch the button on the right side of the meter to "E3D". Which stands for electric field 3 dimensional. For an example of what that looks like see figure 1. Electric fields can be measured two different ways with this meter. The first way is by using a grounding cable (one comes with the meter) to ground the meter.

By grounding the meter, you will gain a true measurement of the electrical field on a 3-dimensional axis. The other way electric fields can be measured using this device is ungrounded. However, if you are not grounding the meter, then you cannot touch it while it is taking measurements. That is because your body acts as an antenna for electric fields and will interfere with the measurement. So, for this measurement to be accurate you must take "potential free" measurements. Which can be difficult to accomplish without the right equipment. In order to take potential free measurements, you must purchase a special clip that goes on the back of the meter. That clip then attaches to a broom stick, which you then hold away from your body at a distance. By holding the broom stick with the meter attached away from your body, you are able to gain a potential free measurement. However, if this sounds like too much work, then simply set the meter on top of the device you are measuring and step away. Or just stick to taking measurements with the meter grounded.

When measuring electric fields, the meter will display the electric field measurement in volts per meter (V/m). Below I have listed the recommended safe levels for electric fields when the meter is grounded. If you fall under "severe problem", you have an electric field problem that needs remediation.

<1 = No problem
1-5 = Slight problem
5-50 = Severe problem
>50 = Extreme problem

For electrical fields that are being measured using the potential free method, below are the recommended safe levels:

<0.3 = No problem
0.3-1.5 = Slight problem
1.5-10 = Severe problem
>10 = Extreme problem

When measuring electric fields using the NFA 1000, it is always a good idea to gain 3 different measurements at varying distances, such as:

1. 1" away
2. 12" or 1' away
3. 36" or 3' away

If you are measuring something with a high electric field such as an electric stove top, hold the meter at varying distances as to where you typically stand while using the stove top. If on average you stand right next to the stove top while it is in use, stand the same distance away with the meter and take your measurements. Also, stand further away and notice the measurements get lower with more distance.

Although this meter is more expensive than the other meters listed, it is one of the best meters I have ever used. If you are thinking about starting your own EMF home inspection business, this meter is a must have for electric and magnetic fields. However, if you are simply looking to see how bad the EMF environment is around your home, a less expensive meter may be used. Unfortunately, at this point I have not found one that I can recommend.

Steps 2 & 3-

Establishing a Baseline

Prior to starting an EMF home inspection, I send each one of my clients a pre inspection checklist. This lets me know before entering their home what the problem areas are. I like to gain a complete understanding of what sort of lifestyle my client has and the pre inspection checklist reveals that. Below I have included the exact questionnaire I use as well as an example of a filled-out version from a client.

Pre-Inspection Form

In order to gain an accurate representation of your current EMF use, whether intentional or unintentional, please fill out the below questionnaire to the best of your ability.

Exterior of House

1. Are there any above ground power lines near your property?

2. Do you have a smart meter? (I.e. gas, electric, water)
3. Can you see a cell tower from anywhere on your property?
4. Do you have solar panels?
5. Are your neighbors' homes close enough to pick up their Wi-Fi?
6. Do you have a wireless security/doorbell system?
7. Do you have any exterior Bluetooth enabled devices? (i.e. pool lighting, anything that can be controlled by an app on your phone)

Interior of House

1. Do you have Wi-Fi?
2. Do you have a range extender for your Wi-Fi?
3. Do you have a cordless home phone?
4. Do you have a voice automated assistant? (i.e. Alexa, Google assistant)
5. Do you turn your cell phone on "airplane mode" when not in use?
6. Do you have a tablet(s)? (i.e. iPad, kindle)
7. Do you have a "smart tv"?
8. Do you have Bluetooth enabled devices? (i.e. stereo/speakers, headphones, keyboard, mouse, printer, rumba vacuum, tile)
9. Do you have a laptop or home computer?
10. Do you have dimmer switches?
11. Do you leave your electronic appliances plugged in when not in use?
12. Do you use a microwave oven?
13. Do you have an electric stove?
14. Do you have fluorescent/halogen light bulbs?
15. Do you use a hair dryer?

16. Do you use an electric razor or electric toothbrush?
17. Do you have "smart appliances"?
18. Do you sleep near a plugged-in lamp?
19. Do you have a plugged-in alarm clock near where you sleep?
20. Has there ever been mold damage in your home?
21. Do you have a Wi-Fi enabled thermostat? (i.e. Nest)
22. Do you use an electric blanket or electric heating pad?
23. Do you have "smart plugs"?
24. Do you have a Wi-Fi or Bluetooth enabled baby monitor?
25. Do you have a Bluetooth enabled air purifier? (i.e. Molekule)
26. Do you have any video game consoles? (i.e. Xbox, Wii, Nintendo switch, PlayStation)
27. Do you have two or more stories in your home?

Personal

1. Do you carry your cell phone on your body?
2. Do you use speakerphone while talking on your cell phone?
3. Do you wear any "smart" devices? (i.e. Apple Watch, fitness tracker, Fitbit)
4. Do you use Bluetooth enabled headphones?
5. Do you have metal fillings?
6. Do you use metal framed glasses?
7. Do you have any metal in your body? (i.e. metal rod, screws)
8. Do you carry any keyless entry devices on

your body? (i.e. car keys)
9. Do you wear a wireless diabetes monitor?
10. Do you have a "smart" or electric car?
11. Do you have Wi-Fi capabilities in your car?
12. Are you using your TV, cell phone, computer or tablet within an hour of falling asleep?

Fill in the blank

1. How many hours a day do you watch television?
2. How many hours a day do you use your cell phone?
3. How many hours a day do you use your computer?
4. How many hours a day do you use your tablet? (i.e. iPad, kindle)
5. How many hours of sleep are you getting per night?
6. Do you have difficulty staying or falling asleep?
7. How long does it take for you to fall asleep?
8. Do you know your body voltage in bed?
9. How many people live in your home?
10. Where is your phone and/or tablet when you are sleeping?
11. How often do you check your cell phone throughout the night?
12. When was the last time you had a home EMF inspection?
13. How many years have you been using a cell phone?
14. How many waking hours per day are you spending technology free?

The intention of the above checklist is to get you thinking of all the EMFs that are currently in your life. Although the list is not fully inclusive, as I do not know your specific situation, it does cover a very large spectrum of average EMF exposure.

Pre-Inspection Form (Filled out by client)

Exterior of House

1. Are there any above ground power lines near your property?
   A. *No. They are buried at the street.*
2. Do you have a smart meter? (I.e. gas, electric, water)
   A. *What is a smart meter?*
3. Can you see a cell tower from anywhere on your property?
   A. *I have no idea what a cell tower looks like.*
4. Do you have solar panels?
   A. *I do and so do all of my neighbors.*
5. Are your neighbors' homes close enough to pick up their Wi-Fi?
   A. *Yes. I can see 16 of my neighbors WiFi.*
6. Do you have a wireless security/doorbell system?
   A. *I have Ring, does that count?*
7. Do you have any exterior Bluetooth enabled devices? (i.e. pool lighting, anything that can be controlled by an app on your phone)
   A. *I have a Bluetooth enabled sprinkler system that I can control from my phone, and my sound bar for my outdoor television. I think that's it.*

Interior of House

1. Do you have Wi-Fi?
   A. *Of course, who doesn't?*
2. Do you have a range extender for your Wi-Fi?
   A. *Yes. I have a large house so it is necessary.*
3. Do you have a cordless home phone?
   A. *No.*
4. Do you have a voice automated assistant? (i.e. Alexa, Google assistant)
   A. *I have an Alexa device in all of the rooms of my house.*
5. Do you turn your cell phone on "airplane mode" when not in use?
   A. *No. Only when I am on an airplane.*
6. Do you have a tablet(s)? (i.e. iPad, kindle)
   A. *I have 2 iPads and my wife has a kindle.*
7. Do you have a "smart tv"?
   A. *Yes. One in all of the bedrooms, living room and outside entertainment area.*
8. Do you have Bluetooth enabled devices? (i.e. stereo/speakers, headphones, keyboard, mouse, printer, rumba vacuum, tile)
   A. *Yes. Sound bars, headphones, keyboard, mouse, printer, tile, and the things that are outside.*
9. Do you have a laptop or home computer?
   A. *Both.*
10. Do you have dimmer switches?
    A. *Yes of course.*
11. Do you leave your electronic appliances plugged in when not in use?
    A. *Only until my wife unplugs them.*
12. Do you use a microwave oven?
    A. *Yes, for breakfast and dinner.*

13. Do you have an electric stove?

    A. *Glass top? Then yes.*

14. Do you have fluorescent/halogen light bulbs?

    A. *Yes.*

15. Do you use a hair dryer?

    A. *No, but my wife does.*

16. Do you use an electric razor or electric toothbrush?

    A. *No.*

17. Do you have "smart appliances"?

    A. *A lot of them.*

18. Do you sleep near a plugged-in lamp?

    A. *Yes, one on each nightstand.*

19. Do you have a plugged-in alarm clock near where you sleep?

    A. *No, I use my phone as my alarm clock.*

20. Has there ever been mold damage in your home?

    A. *Not that I know of.*

21. Do you have a Wi-Fi enabled thermostat? (i.e. Nest)

    A. *Yes, I do.*

22. Do you use an electric blanket or electric heating pad?

    A. *No.*

23. Do you have "smart plugs"?

    A. *Just the one that controls my sprinkler.*

24. Do you have a Wi-Fi or Bluetooth enabled baby monitor?

    A. *No.*

25. Do you have a Bluetooth enabled air purifier? (i.e. Molekule)

    A. *Not that I know of. I have an air purifier but I don't know if it is Bluetooth. It connects to my WiFi.*

26. Do you have any video game consoles? (i.e. Xbox, Wii, Nintendo switch, PlayStation)

    A. *Xbox and Wii.*

27. Do you have two or more stories in your home?

    A. *No, one story.*

Personal

1. Do you carry your cell phone on your body?

   A. *In my pocket.*

2. Do you use speakerphone while talking on your cell phone?

   A. *Sometimes, but not always.*

3. Do you wear any "smart" devices? (i.e. Apple Watch, fitness tracker, Fitbit)

   A. *Apple Watch.*

4. Do you use Bluetooth enabled headphones?

   A. *Yes, apple air pods.*

5. Do you have metal fillings?

   A. *Yes.*

6. Do you use metal framed glasses?

   A. *Yes.*

7. Do you have any metal in your body? (i.e. metal rod, screws)

   A. *Not that I know of.*

8. Do you carry any keyless entry devices on your body? (i.e. car keys)

   A. *Key fob for my car and my wifes.*

9. Do you wear a wireless diabetes monitor?

   A. *No.*

10. Do you have a "smart" or electric car?

    A. *No.*

11. Do you have Wi-Fi capabilities in your car?

    A. *Yes, but I think the free trial expires soon.*

12. Are you using your TV, cell phone, computer or tablet within an hour of falling asleep?

    A. *Every night I watch TV, check my email on my cell phone and then go to sleep. Short answer is yes.*

Fill in the blank

1. How many hours a day do you watch television?

    A. *4 hours*

2. How many hours a day do you use your cell phone?

    A. *6 hours*

3. How many hours a day do you use your computer?

    A. *8 hours or more depending on my work schedule.*

4. How many hours a day do you use your tablet? (i.e. iPad, kindle)

    A. *Maybe an hour total per day. Some days I don't use it at all. On work trips I use it on the plane for the entire flight.*

5. How many hours of sleep are you getting per night?

    A. *4-6 hours.*

6. Do you have difficulty staying or falling asleep?

    A. *Trouble with both.*

7. How long does it take for you to fall asleep?

    A. *Without sleep aids, an hour or so.*

8. Do you know your body voltage in bed?

    A. *What is that?*

9. How many people live in your home?

    A. *4 including me.*

10. Where is your phone and/or tablet when you are sleeping?

    A. *Next to me on the nightstand or under my pillow.*

11. How often do you check your cell phone throughout the night?

    A. *Whenever I get up to use the restroom.*

12. When was the last time you had a home EMF inspection?

    A. *Never, this is my first time.*

13. How many years have you been using a cell phone?

    A. *15 years give or take.*

14. How many waking hours per day are you spending technology free?

    A. *None.*

What I typically look for first in these pre inspections is what their "large sources of radiation" are. For example, in the form above you'll notice that the individual has WiFi, a WiFi range extender, a Ring security doorbell, and solar panels (in my experience, these four items generate the highest amount of EMF radiation inside of a home). When I saw that they had all four of the top largest sources of radiation I knew that the individual knew nothing about EMFs, otherwise their home would not have any of these. These are homes where the largest differences are felt immediately upon remediation.

An additional step that I take as part of the pre inspection is to look up the individual's home on the website: antennasearch.com. This website allows you to see how many cell phone towers there are near your home. Usually the search comes back with a radius of all towers within 2-3 miles. After the search reveals how many towers there are, I like to click on the link that shows the exact locations of the results. Sometimes there may only be 5 towers near the individual's home which in most cases is good, but after clicking on their exact location it could reveal that they are all within 100 feet of the home (which is not good). I will go into further detail about the dangers of living near a cell tower in the radio frequency chapter.

After the checklist has been thoroughly reviewed and my notes are compiled, I set up a time with the client to complete the EMF home inspection. I recommend setting up a time where all individuals living in the home can be in attendance. In the past this had meant working weekends, but with more people working from home it has been easier to conduct the inspection with everyone there.

When I first arrive at the clients' house, I obtain a baseline reading of the property. This step is crucial in order to determine if the changes made later on are beneficial as well as documenting your findings. If at all possible, having a partner to write down your measurements is helpful. On the following pages, I have included a typical documentation sheet that I use for EMF home inspections. You can use it for yourself, or create your own, just make sure to document!

Inspection Form

Client Name: _____ Date: _____

Address: _____ Time: _____

Temperature: _____ Weather: _____

Notes:

_____

_____

Exterior of Property

	Baseline	Inspection	Remediation
Radio Frequency North			
Radio Frequency South			
Radio Frequency East			
Radio Frequency West			
Magnetic Field North			
Magnetic Field South			
Magnetic Field East			
Magnetic Field West			

Electric Field North			
Electric Field South			
Electric Field East			
Electric Field West			
Dirty Electricity North			
Dirty Electricity South			
Dirty Electricity East			
Dirty Electricity West			

Interior of Property

	Baseline	Inspection	Remediation
Radio Frequency Room 1			
Radio Frequency Room 2			
Radio Frequency Room 3			
Radio Frequency Room 4			
Radio			

Frequency Room 5			
Radio Frequency Room 6			
Radio Frequency Room 7			
Radio Frequency Room 8			
Radio Frequency Room 9			
Magnetic Field Room 1			
Magnetic Field Room 2			
Magnetic Field Room 3			
Magnetic Field Room 4			
Magnetic Field Room 5			
Magnetic Field Room 6			
Magnetic Field Room 7			
Magnetic Field Room 8			

DIY EMF HOME INSPECTION GUIDE

Magnetic Field Room 9			
Electric Field Room 1			
Electric Field Room 2			
Electric Field Room 3			
Electric Field Room 4			
Electric Field Room 5			
Electric Field Room 6			
Electric Field Room 7			
Electric Field Room 8			
Electric Field Room 9			
Dirty Electricity Room 1			
Dirty Electricity Room 2			
Dirty Electricity			

Room 3			
Dirty Electricity Room 4			
Dirty Electricity Room 5			
Dirty Electricity Room 6			
Dirty Electricity Room 7			
Dirty Electricity Room 8			
Dirty Electricity Room 9			

The main difference in establishing a baseline and the actual inspection is that during the baseline inspection the source of the problem is not sought after. Instead I tend to focus on the background ambient levels within the area and then during the actual inspection I locate the sources. For example, at one of my clients homes I walked around the inside of his bedroom with my radio frequency meter, pointing it in the direction of each wall as well as standing in the center of his room. The north wall had an average reading 100x higher than the other walls. Rather than determining at that moment what the problem was, I marked it down and then continued to the next room. Since the client was following me, he said "well, aren't you going to investigate the source?" I replied "Not just yet. I want to gain a baseline understanding of what your house is on average before I start trying to fix anything. That way I know if what I am doing is actually working, and have documented proof." The client understood and later after establishing the baseline of his home I went back and started remediating the biggest problem areas first. His room just so happened to have a bank of four smart meters on the exterior north wall that was putting off extremely high levels of radio frequencies. After fixing the problem and showing a zero reading on my meter he asked "what was the reading before again?" Without documenting the baseline reading first, I would have had to remember that information. Instead I had it written down and could show him the before and after readings, proving that there was a problem to begin with.

You would be surprised at how many people fail to complete a baseline reading of a property prior to remediating the problem areas. Establishing a baseline is the best way to determine if what you did worked or not. Plus, later on down the road you have documentation to compare your new readings to. Below I have broken down how to establish a baseline into 5 easy steps. The pre inspection checklist should be completed prior to conducting the baseline measurement but is included in the steps to establish the properties baseline.

Step 1- "Pre inspection checklist"
Have client fill out pre inspection checklist and determine large sources of radiation. Look up clients address on antennasearch.com. Document results.

Step 2- "Initial documentation"
Upon arrival make sure to note the date, time, weather/temperature, and anything out of the ordinary. For example: January 1, 2020, 9:00AM, very dark clouds but no rain 80 degrees, trees leaning onto power lines outside of house.

Step 3- "Exterior of the property"
I always greet the client first and then explain to them that I am going to start establishing baseline readings of the property. I invite them to join me if they would like but depending on their circumstances they may just want to sit and watch from afar. This is where the fun begins.

I begin with my radio frequency meter first and do a thorough walk through around the perimeter of the property making sure to point the meter at the house as well as the neighbors' homes. Typically, the backyard is fenced off so I ask for the client to unlock the fence while I am documenting the other sides of the home. That way when I get to the backyard I can walk freely around and gain my measurements. On most homes the exterior of the property isn't the problem, but gaining a baseline reading is crucial either way. To make things easier on myself, I usually break the house up into North/South/East/West, but if you are unfamiliar with coordinating yourself that way then I suggest using the following: Front of house, back of house, left side, right side. Either way make sure to take readings on each of the sides of the home and document your findings. Since the findings may range from high to low numbers, I will more often than not, document the highest number read on the meter as well as the lowest in the baseline column of the inspection form. For example:

Radio Frequency North:
 1. 10 μW/m^2 (Low)
 2. 1,800 μW/m^2 (High)

After walking around the entire property with my radio frequency meter, I then switch to my next meter. It is completely up to you which order you use the meters in, but I typically stick to the following order:

 1. Radio Frequency Meter
 2. Magnetic Field Meter
 3. Electric Field Meter
 4. Dirty Electricity Meter

Using my magnetic field meter, I follow the same process of walking around the perimeter of the exterior of the home I am inspecting. Making sure to document my findings on the North, South, East, and West sides of the property. If I notice any unusual spikes of measurements on the meter, notes are written down on a scratch piece of paper. However, the main goal at this point is only to gain a baseline "average" reading of the property.

Next, I walk take out my electric field meter and follow the same process as above, only with one main difference. In order to gain a true measurement of the electric field around the property, the meter itself must be grounded. For this, I take out my grounding rod, find an area where the dirt is easily penetrated, and shove the rod into the ground. The wire attached to the rod is then inserted into the meter, making it grounded and therefore capable of accurately measuring the electric fields around the property. Some individuals do not use the grounding method for their inspections, but I have found the measurements more accurate when grounding the meter. In the electrical field inspection chapter, we will go over this in further detail.

Once the electric field meter is properly grounded, there is one limitation: distance. The cable attached to the grounding rod reaches around 10 ft, making it difficult to walk around the entire property. Therefore, the best way to complete this part of the baseline inspection is to take measurements 10 ft at a time, then move the grounding rod and continue onward.

The fourth meter used during the baseline inspection of the exterior of the property is the dirty electricity meter. This only applies however, if there are outlets on the exterior of the property. This is due to the fact that the meter itself needs to be plugged into an outlet to gain its reading. Usually, there are 2 outlets that I have come across on the exterior of the property. One near the front door and one near the back door. For this baseline measurement, all that needs to be done is: find the outlet, plug in the meter, write down the baseline measurement.

After walking around the perimeter of the exterior of the property, and writing down the baseline measurements, next I head inside. Although you may want to start making changes and remediating the problem areas at this point, I strongly recommend waiting until later to do so. The reason being, if you make a change to the exterior of the property, it could affect the readings of the interior of the property prior to establishing a baseline. By waiting until the baseline measurements of the exterior and interior are gathered, you will know exactly if one area directly affects another through remediation.

Step 4- "Interior of the property"
When starting on the interior of the property, the first thing I do is make sure that all of the individuals in the home have their phones switched to "airplane mode". When their phones are on airplane mode, I also make sure that the options for WiFi and Bluetooth are switched off. Some clients have asked why and I simply show them the radiation coming off of their phones by using my radio frequency meter. Once they are aware that their device is putting off radiation and could interfere with gaining a true measurement of the environment, they always comply and turn their phones on airplane mode.

Following the same pattern as the exterior of the home, I establish a baseline of the interior of the home by moving from room to room using only one meter at a time. However, rather than breaking down the property into North, South, East and West, I document the interior of the property by room. For example, most homes today consist of 3 bedrooms, 2 bathrooms, a kitchen, dining room, family room, and garage. Bringing the total "rooms" to 9. By breaking up the interior measurements by room, it makes finding the source of the problem later on easier.

To make things easier, I start with the room closest to the front door and work in a clockwise pattern around the interior of the property. On a scratch piece of paper, I will document what each room is. See below for example:

Room 1- Family room
Room 2- Kitchen
Room 3- Dining Room
Room 4- Bedroom #1
Room 5- Bathroom #1
Room 6- Master Bedroom
Room 7- Master Bathroom
Room 8- Bedroom #2
Room 9- Garage

Starting with room number 1 (family room), I follow the same order of meters as the exterior of the property by using the radio frequency meter. I walk around the entire perimeter of that room, pointing the meter at the walls, at any devices that may be emitting radiation, and document the highest reading as well as the lowest for that room. Remember, at this point we are just gathering a baseline measurement, so do not make any changes to the room.

Once room number 1 is complete, I then move to the next room, using the same radio frequency meter. In the past I tried multiple ways of establishing a baseline, some involved switching meters and doing only one room at a time. However, by sticking with one meter at a time, it makes documentation easier.

After completing all 9 rooms (or more/less depending on the size of the home), I return back to room number 1 and start the process all over again with meter number 2. Which for me means the magnetic field meter. I then walk around each room, making sure to cover each and every inch. Unlike the radio frequency baseline inspection, I also flip light switches on and off in each room while using the meter. Sometimes, this has led to the discovery of wiring problems that results in higher magnetic field readings.

Further detail will be provided in the actual inspection portion of this guide, but for now you are mainly looking to gain a baseline reading of each room.

Once the magnetic field baseline readings are completed for the 9 rooms, I then return back to room number 1 and begin again with meter number 3, the electric field meter. However, I tend to not actually use the electric field meter for gathering measurements on the interior of the property. Instead, I use my body as the meter by using my body voltage meter to gain measurements. For me, this has proven to be a faster way at gaining a more accurate measurement of the electric field within a property.

First, I check to make sure that the outlet I am going to use is grounded with a miniature ground outlet tester. Once it has been determined that the outlet is properly grounded, I then plug the body voltage meter into the ground portion of the outlet, and begin walking around the entire room, slowly, with my body voltage meter. What it is measuring is the amount of electricity flowing through my body due to the electric fields present in the room. Like the magnetic field baseline inspection, I also flip light switches on and off to gain an accurate baseline measurement.

One further step I take with the body voltage meter is that I actually sit down on the couches, beds, chairs, or whatever else is set up inside the various rooms. This lets me know how much electricity is flowing through my client's body while they are in bed, or simply sitting on the couch or kitchen table. Later on, in the actual inspection portion, I investigate the electric field problems further by using the electric field meter. But for now, remember, the goal is just to establish a baseline.

Lastly, after finishing up with the 9 room baseline measurement of electric fields/body voltage, I return back to room number 1 and begin measuring the dirty electricity. Starting in the first room, plug the dirty electricity meter into each outlet within the room, documenting the highest levels of dirty electricity as well as the lowest. Then move to the next room and so on, until you have gained a baseline measurement of each of the 9 rooms.

After completing the interior baseline measurements, you may want to start the full inspection immediately, but I strongly urge you to continue on to step 5 in order to ensure proper documentation has been completed.

Step 5- "Go over documentation"
For good measure, I include a step where going over the baseline documentation is the main purpose. I do this even if the client followed me throughout the entire inspection, witnessing the results for

themselves. This ensures that both the client and I are on the same page as to the readings and it also provides an opportunity to explain in detail what will be occurring during the actual inspection.

Like I have said before, so far this is merely a baseline inspection of the property and not the actual inspection. The actual inspection will be broken down into full chapters to follow. In the meantime, your primary concern should be to double check that you have a baseline measurement for the entire exterior and interior of the property. Without it documented, once the inspection and remediation start, you won't know if the work that you have done was successful.

It is a good idea at this point to go over the documentation with the client. If you are doing an inspection of your own home, then I strongly encourage you to go over the baseline results with someone you trust. Show them all of the measurements you have obtained before starting the actual inspection and remediation. I have found this step to be extremely helpful at holding people accountable for proper documentation.

In the following chapters you will learn how to conduct an EMF home inspection after obtaining your baseline measurement of the property in question.

Steps 4 & 5-

Radio Frequency Inspection and Remediation

At this point you should have completed your baseline measurements of the property. If you have not, please go back and read steps 2 and 3, *Establishing a Baseline.*

When I am completing a home inspection for a client I will more often than not start out with measuring radio frequencies. I do this because radio frequencies have consistently been the major problem at all of the homes I have visited. There hasn't been a single home in which I have visited that didn't have at least one radio frequency emitting device putting off extremely unsafe levels of radiation. For example, the standard home in which I conduct home inspections has at least one "smart" television, WiFi router, or a smart meter. In one of my client's homes however, they had 5 smart televisions with 5 separate smart voice enabled remotes, 3 smart meters due to having solar panels on their home, 2 WiFi routers, a WiFi range extender, and multiple Bluetooth devices all operating on high radio frequency levels. The client initially had been complaining of severe migraines whenever he arrived home from work and had been having difficulty concentrating on the easiest of tasks—like forgetting where certain dishes went in his kitchen or completely forgetting what his wife said seconds after she said it. After pulling out my radio frequency meter and "making the invisible radiation, visible", he immediately knew that his house was the problem. What further solidified that for him was when we remediated his environment and eliminated all of the sources of radio frequency radiation. Within minutes his migraines went away and haven't returned to this day. At the end of the inspection he said "I never knew that my smart devices were a problem, they don't tell you that when you buy them. They should come with a label that says: warning-may cause headaches and forgetfulness." Unfortunately, his story is not unique as I have found that many more people are complaining of "phantom headaches/migraines" whenever they are at home for prolonged periods of time. Luckily, in this chapter you will learn the 3 steps to conducting your own radio frequency inspection. Below I have broken those 3 steps down into easy to understand segments with examples and pictures. After that you will learn how to remediate any radio frequency problems you may have in the remediation section.

Before we get started on conducting a radio frequency inspection, understanding what they are is crucial. Understanding what you are inspecting is fundamental to the success of the inspection itself. Simply put, radio frequencies are data packed signals that are transferred through the air from one point to another. All wireless technology devices work through invisible frequencies called radio frequencies traveling through the air. For example, when you send a text message from your cell phone to another cell phone, think about how it gets there. There are no wires connecting the two cell phones, so how does the text message instantly travel from one place to another? It takes the text message, turns it into a frequency and then travels invisibly through the air, eventually making its way to its intended destination. Imagine explaining that to someone 50 years ago.

Regarding safe levels of radio frequencies, there technically aren't any. We as humans were not designed to be around pulsed radio frequency wireless radiation. Therefore, I usually recommend that anything wireless be avoided at all costs. However, that is not likely in today's world and therefore below I have included the recommended safe levels by the top experts on the matter, Building Biologists as well as the current levels set by the FCC.

1. 10,000,000 $\mu W/m^2$= FCC
2. .1 $\mu W/m^2$= Building Biologists

The most common sources of Radio Frequency radiation can best be understood by breaking them down into two separate categories: Exterior and Interior.

*Most common **exterior** sources*

1. Smart Meters (Gas, Electric, Water)
2. Ring Doorbell
3. Neighbors WiFi

4. Cell Phone Towers

*Most common **interior** sources*

1. WiFi router
2. WiFi range extender
3. Smart Television
4. Smart Television Remote
5. Cell phones
6. Bluetooth devices
7. Smart appliances

If you are one of those individuals that has all of the above exterior and interior sources of radio frequency radiation, then pay careful attention to the steps listed below for inspecting your home. Chances are, you may have additional sources of radio frequency radiation as the list above is only the most common sources and not all of them.

Below I have broken down what you will be doing during the radio frequency inspection portion of the EMF home inspection. The following 3 steps will be discussed in detail throughout the chapter:

Step 1- Establish Baseline
Step 2- Exterior of the property
Step 3- Interior of the property

Step 1- Establish Baseline

By now you should have done a walk-through of the exterior and interior of the property, and established a baseline measurement of the radio frequencies present. On the inspection form, the column labeled "baseline" should be completely filled out. If it is not completed, moving on to step 2 of the radio frequency inspection is not advised.

Step 2- Exterior of the property

Similarly to the baseline inspection, you will head outside to the exterior of the property with your radio frequency meter (HF-35C) in hand. Here is where you will begin the inspection. Starting out at the front of the house, and with the meter on, begin walking around the entire front exterior area. Point the meter at the house, at the street, and anywhere located near the front of the property. If the meter reading goes up, follow it. Act as if the meter is a metal detector and you are searching for a piece of buried metal. Move towards the higher readings, trying to locate the source. In many cases you will find that the source of the higher readings coming from the front of the house is related to something radiating from the interior of the property. However, on some occasions you will pick up your neighbors WiFi, or even worse, you will have a radio frequency wireless radiation emitting device, like a Ring doorbell, situated near your front door. If that is the case, document on the "inspection column" of the inspection form the source of the problem, as well as the readings on your meter. If by chance your meter readings are extremely high all over the exterior of the property, check your antennasearch.com results. More often than not, in the case of an extremely high reading all over the exterior of the property, a cell tower is nearby. For example, one of my clients was looking to purchase a home on a plot of land outside of civilization. It was in a remote area and sat on almost 20 acres of vacant land. Near the back of the property was a house and behind the house was a mountain. On the antennasearch.com results, the nearest cell tower was located 2.94 miles away. From those results alone, I originally thought that the place would be far enough away that the house wouldn't be affected by the radio frequency radiation coming from the cell tower. But I was wrong. Arriving at the location to complete a "move-in" EMF home inspection, I immediately noticed that I could see the cell tower, almost 3 miles away, towering over any structure nearby. The exterior readings on that property were amongst the highest readings I had ever read, and therefore I recommended that my client continue searching for another home. A good rule of thumb to live by in regards to radio frequency radiation and cell towers is: if you can see a cell tower from anywhere on your property, chances are it's affecting you. However, using a meter to verify the validity of that statement is always recommended. Currently, my house is situated less than 2 miles from a cell tower. Yet, due to various houses in between my house and the cell tower, the exterior readings of the property are at zero. So, as you can see, distance isn't the only factor to consider when it comes to cell towers. If there are buildings or houses in between, those buildings or houses may be blocking the radiation from reaching your property.

Once you have searched the entire front of the property with your radio frequency meter and written down all of your findings on the inspection form, move to the side of the property and continue your search. Point the meter everywhere you can, trying to find any sources of possible radio frequency radiation. Typically, on the sides of properties you will get readings from neighbors WiFi and/or smart meters. See below for what a smart meter looks like:

In the picture above one of the smart meters has a cover over it (far right) and the one in the middle is not covered. A smart meter is basically a device that measures your electricity usage within your home on a constant basis while transmitting that usage to your utility company. Which means that your utility company knows what devices you are using inside of your home, when you are using them, and the exact duration of how long you use them. Think of your smart meter as a cell phone, and every time you open the refrigerator, flip on a light switch, turn on your television, etc., your smart meter sends a "text message" to your utility company letting them know what you are doing. The utility company is very open about this and have nicknamed it "data collection." The information that they collect is then sold to third parties who use that information to try and sell you things based off of the devices you mainly use within your home. However, that's not what you should be worried about. What you should be worried about is the constant radio frequency radiation coming from the smart meter on the exterior of your home. If you live in a house, they are usually located on the side of the garage near your breaker box. If you live in an apartment they tend to be located in a "bank" area near the ground floor. If you are friends with your neighbors, I also recommend that you try and locate where their smart meter is in relation to your home. On most occasions, my clients remediate their neighbors' homes if their levels are affecting the exterior of their home.

After completing the front and sides of the property, next head into the backyard with your radio frequency meter. Typically, the main problem areas you will run into are from the WiFi on the interior of the property as well as neighbors WiFi, but on more rare occasions you will encounter Bluetooth devices in the backyard. Some people may have Bluetooth cameras, others have Bluetooth speakers, and if there is a pool, they may have Bluetooth devices that control the settings or the color of the lights within the pool. In those cases, make sure to turn the devices on an off, gathering measurements of both. In most cases, if it is Bluetooth, it will have high measurements even if it is off.

After completing the inspection of the exterior of the property, you should have gathered the areas that need to be fixed, or "remediated." However, do not take any remediation steps yet. Document the areas that need to be remediated (i.e. smart meter, Ring doorbell, etc.) and head inside the property to complete the interior portion of the radio frequency inspection.

Below are some examples of cell phone towers located on the exterior of the property. One of them is disguised as a palm tree, but do not be fooled, they are just as dangerous as a standard one.

Step 3- Interior of the property

With your radio frequency meter in hand, walk through the interior of the property room by room, starting at room number 1. Walk through the room, pointing the meter at every wall, the ceiling and the floor, making sure to cover every inch. If the meter reading "spikes", follow the spiked reading until you find the source. Once the source is located, write it down in the inspection portion under radio frequency room number 1. In most of the homes that I inspect, room number 1 is the family room and tend to be the largest problem area. What you are looking for is anything that is labeled "smart" or "wireless." If the home has a smart television, turn it on and off, getting measurements of both. If the television isn't smart, the readings will be zero. If the remote is a smart remote with voice activation, point it at the meter and push any of the buttons (this one will shock you at how high it is). Most standard remotes will have a zero reading. If there is a cable box, make sure to turn it on and off, checking and documenting the readings of both. Cable boxes today are run on "RF signals" aka radio frequency signals. These boxes transmit extremely high levels of radio frequencies, even while in the off position.

After getting measurements of those few items in room number 1 (family room), move onto the next room with your radio frequency meter. Room number 2 is typically the kitchen and this is where the WiFi router is more often than not located.

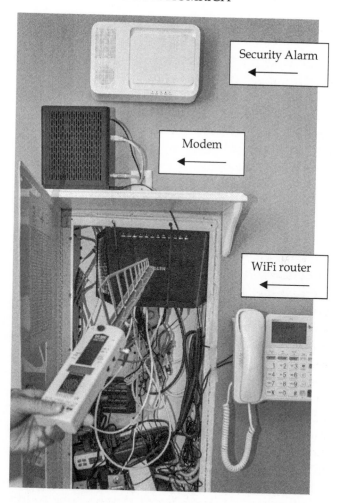

Most of the readings inside that room will come from the WiFi router but here is where I like to have fun and reveal another huge source of radiation. The microwave. In almost every home I have ever done an inspection on, there has been a microwave proudly displayed in the kitchen. If my client is with me, I ask them how often they use the microwave and get responses that vary from "breakfast and dinner", to "I use it as often as I can, it's so fast and convenient." Then I ask how close they stand to it while it's "warming" up their food. Responses vary from 1 foot to 5 feet away. These are the same individuals that contact me for extreme headaches, lack of concentration/brain fog, and inability to sleep. I then have a long conversation about how unhealthy the food is that comes out of a microwave, but I'll let you do the research on that one. After that, I set up a little bit of an experiment with the client. I have them fill up a glass of water, place it inside of the microwave, and walk as far away as possible from the device. I then ask them to press start and turn the microwave on. From across the room, the meter spikes to levels so high that my meter can't read it. Their faces are always in awe at the results. The furthest reading I was able to get was over 30 feet away, and if I had more room then that I'm sure it would have gone further.

The little mesh lining on the inside of the glass door of the microwave is claimed to block radio frequency radiation, but clearly it does not. There hasn't been a single microwave that I have done this experiment on that hasn't put off outrageous radio frequency levels. At that point in the inspection I usually then say "microwave radiation is the same thing as radio frequency radiation. Your cell phone is a microwave, your smart television is a microwave. All of your Bluetooth devices are microwaves. You wouldn't put your ear up to a microwave for hours on end, so why do it with a cell phone?"

Inside of the kitchen there may also be smart

refrigerators and various other smart devices. Gain measurements, document them, and move on to the next room. Room by room make sure to check every inch of the interior of the property. Looking for anything that makes the readings on the meter exceed safe levels. Make sure to point the meter at the walls as well, due to the fact that radio frequency radiation can penetrate through them. If you know where the smart meter is on the exterior of the house, try to find where it is located on the interior of the house in order to see if the radiation penetrates through (it will).

Once you have completed the entire interior of the property, located all of the sources of wireless radio frequency radiation, the next thing to do, prior to remediation is ensure that all of the inspection column on the inspection form is filled out. After making sure your documentation is in order, next you will be remediating the sources of the problem areas.

Remediation

For radio frequency remediation, the goal isn't to get rid of all the technology within the client's home. Rather, it is to set up the technology in a way that it is safe to use. For example, one of the major items I have my clients remove from their home is WiFi. Removing WiFi does not mean removing internet, it merely means removing the wireless component and opting for the safer, faster, more reliable "wired" option of ethernet enabled internet. Somewhere along the line, people forgot all about ethernet and thought that WiFi was the only way to access the internet. I had one client that was very upset when I said that we were going to eliminate the wireless radio frequency radiation within her home by getting rid of WiFi. Being that she worked from home she replied "well how am I supposed to use the internet then? I need the internet to work and pay my bills." I replied "you won't lose the internet or your ability to work at all. We are setting you up with ethernet connectivity, which is just a wired version of accessing the internet. It's not only faster and more reliable than WiFi, but it's safer in regards to radiation." By explaining that there is an alternative option to connect to the internet besides WiFi and then setting it up for the client, I was able to provide her with a safer way to use her technology and not eliminating it all together.

So far you have learned what to look for in regards to radio frequencies during an inspection, but below you will learn the most important part, remediation. Once you have located the sources of radio frequency radiation, your next goal is to eliminate them or get them as close to zero as possible. Due to the fact that your home may vary in its remediation needs, I used the most common sources of radio frequencies as a guide for the remediation steps. As a reminder, here are the most common exterior and interior sources of radio frequency radiation:

*Most common **exterior** sources*

1. Smart Meters (Gas, Electric, Water)
2. Ring Doorbell
3. Neighbors WiFi
4. Cell Phone Towers

*Most common **interior** sources*

1. WiFi router
2. WiFi range extender
3. Smart Television
4. Smart Television Remote
5. Cell phones
6. Bluetooth devices
7. Smart appliances

Exterior remediation "smart meters"-

Smart meters used to be one of the more difficult sources of radiation to remediate. Mainly because nearly every single home in the United States has one. Meaning, if you remove one from a client's home, their neighbor more than likely will still have one. And if their smart meter is facing your client's home, chances are it is radiating towards it as well. Unless you are close with your neighbors and can have them remove theirs as well, alternative methods for remediation may be necessary. Below I have broken down the three main ways smart meter radiation can be remediated.

1. Opt out- If you contact your utility company and tell them that you want to "opt out" of your smart meter, they will come out and switch it for an analog meter. These are the meters that you may remember from 20 years ago. They still measure your utility usage, but they do not operate using radio frequency radiation. Making them safe to have on the exterior of your property. The only downside to having an analog meter on your house is

that your utility company charges you an additional $10.00 per month (on average) as a convenience fee. Although, that may seem like a lot over time, how much is your health worth?

2. Smart Meter Guard- For those of you that do not wish to opt out, or for some reason cannot opt out (renting house or live in apartment), the next best option is a smart meter guard (see picture on page 66). Now, there are many of these guards on the market, available on Amazon, but not all of them are created equal. Make sure to read the reviews as well as check to see if there is a return policy before purchasing. They range from $50.00- $250.00 but the price doesn't reflect its value. Meaning, just because you purchase one that is more expensive, doesn't mean its going to work better. A smart meter guard is basically a metal mesh enclosure that slips over the smart meter and blocks a certain percentage of the radiation strength. It doesn't block everything, only a certain percentage. I would honestly say that it blocks about 90% of the radiation on average if installed correctly.

3. Faraday paint- The radiation coming from the smart meter is so powerful that it makes its way into the inside of the home. Some experts have made claims that the steel enclosure that the smart meter is located in, blocks the radiation from coming into the inside of the home. However, I have yet to find a home where that statement was true. Every home that I have done an inspection for has had radiation coming through their wall from their

smart meter. That is why I always recommend painting the wall on the other side of the smart meter with a special radio frequency blocking paint called "yshield", also known as "faraday paint." The only complaint I have received is that it is expensive. In that case, I created an alternative "cheap" option. For those individuals who cannot afford the $250.00 price tag of the radio frequency blocking paint, the next best option is tinfoil. I know it might sound crazy but it works. Unfortunately, it isn't the most attractive option. So, what you do to combat both price and attractiveness is the following: Get a large framed picture, approximately 3 feet by 3 feet or larger if possible. On the backside of the picture, line it with the tinfoil (sometimes multiple layers are necessary). Then hang the picture on the opposite side of the smart meter, hiding the tinfoil behind the picture. In the cases where I have done this, a reduction in radiation has dropped from unsafe levels to safe levels...with tinfoil.

Exterior remediation "Ring doorbell"-

Although the idea behind a security camera doorbell is a good one, the radiation levels make it unsafe. If you come across a home with a wireless Ring doorbell, the best option is to get rid of it all together. Unfortunately, these devices do not have a wired option and emit levels of radio frequency radiation higher than most meters can read. If you are worried about the security of your home and family, that is understandable and therefore opting for a wired security camera is the safer route to go. The wiring can be hidden inside of the wall, so no wires are showing, and you will still be able to monitor your home and family. There are even some companies that will set up security cameras around your home for free with purchase of their security cameras.

Exterior remediation "Neighbors WiFi"-

If you were to go onto your cell phone or computer and try to connect to WiFi, how many of your neighbors WiFi show up? On average, the homes I conduct inspections for have a minimum of 20 WiFi connectivity options from all over their neighborhood. WiFi is designed to penetrate through walls, which means that your neighbors WiFi is most likely radiating the interior and exterior of your home. If that is the case, and your radio frequency levels are high on the exterior of your home, your only option is to communicate with your neighbors. Unfortunately, you can't put up an EMF protection bubble around the exterior of your property. Sad as it may be, if your home has high exterior radio frequencies coming from sources you cannot remediate, you may have to move. One of my clients had neighbors with extremely high radio frequencies coming from their WiFi router. After trying everything to block the frequencies from coming into her home, she eventually went to her neighbor's house with a meter and explained the situation. That same day, the neighbors moved their WiFi router to the other side of the house, and the radiation levels on the exterior and interior of her property dropped to zero. If you do not have neighbors that are willing to help in your journey to becoming wireless radio frequency radiation free, get them a copy of this guide. Until then my advice to those clients that have somewhat unsafe levels in their backyards or exteriors of their property, is to limit your exposure. Try not to spend the majority of your time outdoors if it is high. Your body will thank you years from now.

Exterior remediation "cell phone towers"-

Living near a cell phone tower, the exterior of the property is nearly impossible to remediate. However, it can be done. One individual in the UK actually built a cinderblock wall that was over 50 feet tall that blocked the radio frequency radiation from a cell tower that was very close to her home. She invested in the wall because she had children who play outside, and didn't want them getting radiated while doing so. The sad part is that a short time after spending thousands of her own money to build the wall, an additional cell tower was put up near the side of the wall. Her story was so unbelievable, that she was actually on the news in the UK. If building your own wall out of cinderblocks is not feasible, then there really isn't any other option for blocking radio frequencies on the exterior of your property. However, if you are one of those individuals who doesn't use the exterior of your property all that much, then you may not have to move. Look up your home on antennasearch.com, figure out how close the cell towers are, if any new ones are planning on going up in the near future, where the new ones are going to be located, and make a decision. Since most of my clients enjoy the outdoors, moving has been some of their only options to avoid the radiation from the cell towers near their home. Just like living near a powerline has been proven to lower a home's value, living near a cell tower will soon be the same.

Interior remediation "WiFi Routers"-

Everyone has WiFi now a days, but the sad truth is that nobody has been able to prove that it is safe. There are however, studies that prove it is not. Unfortunately, as of today there is no way to provide safe wireless internet. Below I have broken down the various options for those who are interested in living a healthier lifestyle by going wired as well as those who are not yet fully ready to get rid of their WiFi.

1. WiFi timer- Think of the timers that you would use during the holidays on your exterior decoration lighting. You set it for x number of hours, and then it turns off. Then it turns back on the next day at that same time, for the same number of hours. These timers are what you would set your WiFi router on. So rather than having your WiFi on 24/7, you would set a time frame where it would be on from. Prior to my clients going completely WiFi free, some of them have simply set a timer where their WiFi turns off at 10:00pm and then turns back on at 6:00am. Which gives them a full 8 hours free of wireless radio frequency radiation. After a few weeks of this, every single one of my clients ends up going to an ethernet connection for their internet because the sleep they are getting while the WiFi is off is "so much more deep and better" than they are used to. If you are not interested in spending the money on a timer for your

WiFi, then my suggestion would be to unplug it at a set time every night because honestly you don't need it while you sleep.

2. Ethernet- A lot of my clients have no clue what this type of connectivity is. So, what I do is flip the WiFi router over, and show them the 4 or 5 ethernet ports on the back of the router. I explain to them that a wire plugs into the back of the router and then the other end plugs into the device being used. Then they understand. However, just because an ethernet wire is plugged in, that doesn't mean the wireless option is disabled on the router. Here is where having a radio frequency meter comes in handy. On some WiFi routers there is a button with the WiFi symbol on it. By clicking that button or holding it down in some cases, the WiFi becomes disabled. However, not all routers are that simple. Most of the newer routers do not come with the button option. Instead you are required to log into your router by typing the IP address (located on the bottom of your router) into an internet browser and de-selecting the option for WiFi. If that is the case for you, make sure to de-select the options for 2.4ghz and 5ghz. After doing so, the WiFi router will no longer have WiFi capability, the WiFi lights will be off on the router, and you will be able to start the ethernet connectivity process.

If your home was built prior to 2016, you may already have ethernet inside of your walls, which saves you a lot of time and money. However, after 2016 most homes being built stopped wiring for ethernet because everyone was using WiFi. If your home is not wired for ethernet, there are numerous companies that will come out to your home and wire everything for ethernet connectivity. They will wire everything, hiding all the wires inside of the walls as well as installing outlets/ports wherever you need internet inside your home. If you are someone who doesn't care about hiding the wiring inside of the walls, you can run a long ethernet cable from your router to your devices for connectivity. But remember, the WiFi option must be turned off, otherwise you will still be radiating yourself with radio frequencies. The price range can vary drastically with getting your house set up for ethernet connectivity, ranging anywhere from $1,000 to $5,000. That price range is mainly labor, because the cost of the ethernet cabling is very cheap. If that price scares you, run the wires around your house yourself, try out how you feel with wired internet, and after you feel the benefits yourself, decide whether investing in hiding the cables is worth it. When you do have someone install ethernet in your home, make sure that they are licensed and insured and that they provide you with a receipt. In some cases, I have had clients write their EMF remediation expenses off on their taxes as an expense for setting up a "home office."

Interior remediation "WiFi range extender"-

These devices are getting more and more common in

the homes that I am inspecting. The excuse I hear as to why they are needed is mostly "I don't get good enough WiFi in certain parts of my house, so I need it." My answer is always "no, you don't." By installing ethernet in your home, you won't need to worry about connectivity issues anywhere inside your home. Wherever there is an ethernet cable, you will have lightning fast internet that is not only faster but more reliable and even better it's safer. If you have a WiFi range extender, get rid of it and get the house wired for ethernet connectivity instead.

Interior remediation "smart televisions"-

The introduction of the smart television is a more recent invention. Unfortunately, as you will soon learn, anything that has the title "smart" operates on radio frequencies, therefore making the devices potentially harmful. If you have a television that is "smart" there are a few things that you can do to remediate the problem. If the steps below are too much at the current moment, the best option you can do is to leave it unplugged while it is not in use.

1. Connect to Ethernet- If you have a smart television, chances are that an ethernet port is located on the backside. If that is the case, connect an ethernet cable to the back of the television and then make sure the other end is connected to your router. If you are adding ethernet to your entire home, make sure to have the electrician install an outlet near the back of your television. This will make the process a lot easier. Once the television has been plugged into ethernet, go into the

settings on the television and deactivate the wireless option and then select the wired option. If you are unfamiliar with getting to the settings page of your television, go onto your computer and look up the user manual of your specific television. There are even sites now that teach you how to deactivate the wireless option on your specific television.

2. Deactivate Wireless Option- Some televisions allow you to completely disable the wireless option, others do not. If you are fortunate enough to have a television that does, then this step will apply. Go into your settings, deactivate the wireless option, and rather than watch shows that are streamed through the internet, set up a non-smart, basic DVD player. This is what a lot of my clients choose to do. Or, Netflix allows you to download movies and shows directly onto your computer. You then can upload the shows you want onto a flash drive and plug that into the back of your television and enjoy.

3. Replace Television- If none of the above options lower the amount of radio frequency radiation, then the only option left is to replace your smart television for one that is not smart. Typically, they are available on eBay for half the price of a smart television and are of the same quality. One of my clients chose this option and then purchased an adapter to connect their laptop to their television. They plug their laptop into the ethernet port nearest the television, then plug the laptop directly into the television and watch their shows that way. It may seem like a lot just to watch

television, but it is one of the safest options you can do.

Interior remediation "smart television remote"-

The remote that comes with most of the smart televisions is equipped with "voice activation". Meaning that you press a button that looks like a microphone, say what you want to watch, and the television plays it. In theory, that sounds amazing right? Well, it actually puts off enormously high levels of radio frequency radiation in doing so. Even with the remote idle, every 10 to 20 seconds, the remote emits a pulse of radio frequency radiation, higher than most of the televisions. If you are doing an inspection and notice one of these remotes, make sure to test it thoroughly. If you discover that it is putting off high levels of radio frequency radiation there is only one thing that you can do to fix the problem.

Replace the remote with a basic universal remote from Walmart or Amazon. Most of the universal remotes that I purchase for clients range from $5.00-$15.00 and can be programmed in a matter of seconds. After replacing the unsafe smart remote, make sure to take out the batteries and place the remote in the garbage. One of my clients took the batteries out of his smart remote, and then sold the remote on eBay. That in turn, paid for his new universal remote and then some.

Interior remediation "cell phones"-

Cell phones are some of the worst culprits of high radio frequency radiation. They constantly pulse radio frequency signals back and forth to the nearest cell tower, making sure that the device has a signal. On top of that, any applications that are running on the device in the background have a tendency to pulse radio frequency signals as well. Most "smart" phones today even have a warning in the legal section of the user manual stating that the user should not use the phone against the body. Feel free to look in your user manual. However, most of these warnings are in reference to the SAR rating or Specific Absorption Rate. Which has nothing to do with the radio frequency exposure. Unfortunately, that rating has been the same since the early 1990's and hasn't been updated since. Rather than setting limits on if the phone heats the brain (SAR), limits should be set on the radio frequency levels emanating from the device. Currently, the exposure limits set are millions of times higher than the levels proven to cause harm. If you suffer from headaches, tinnitus and have concentration issues, and your cell phone is putting off high levels of radio frequency radiation on your meter, then the following remediation steps could potentially help.

1. Airplane mode- The problem isn't the cell phone itself, it's the radiation it emits while trying to connect during a phone call, searching the web, sending a text message or playing games. Even with it idle, it is emitting high levels of radiation. Think about the people who carry their phones in their pockets or bras and then think about the vital organs near them. Do you really want radio frequency radiation near your genitals or heart, etc.? When the phone is in your pocket

and you receive a phone call, the radiation spikes. Could that be dangerous? Currently there are no scientific studies that have proven it is safe to carry your phone on your body, and even the manufacturer warns against it in the user manual. With that being said, there is a safe way to carry your phone on you — using airplane mode. If you switch your phone onto airplane mode, disconnect the WiFi and Bluetooth option, then carrying your phone on your body becomes safe. That is in 99% of the clients I have tested. However, there have been a few phones that still emit radiation while in airplane mode. If that is the case, you may need to swap your phone out for another model. But make sure to bring your radio frequency meter with you when doing so. That way you can test the levels while in airplane mode. Also, while the phone is in airplane mode, you can still use most of your applications, the alarm, and even your maps. For directions, simply enter the address where you wish to go, load the map, hit start, and then switch the phone over to airplane mode. It will then direct you how to get to where you are going in a safer way without the radio frequency radiation.

Before I chose to get rid of my cell phone all together, I made it a point to turn my phone off of airplane mode once an hour to load emails, text messages, and anything else I needed. Then I would switch it back onto airplane mode, read my messages, type out a response, turn it back off of airplane mode, send the responses, then return the phone back to airplane mode for another hour. This may be difficult at first, but limiting your cell phone use will eventually leave you feeling more like "you." At night while you are sleeping, your phone should also be on airplane mode. Remember, your alarm will still work even if the phone is on airplane mode.

2. Ethernet adapter- For those of you that need to be in constant contact with your family or friends, then this remediation step is for you. There are now adapters available for you to use your phone using an ethernet connection. While the phone is on airplane mode, it will not receive phone calls or text messages. However, with an ethernet adapter (available on amazon and shown below on the right) you will be able to plug your phone directly into your router and use it without the radio frequency radiation. You will then be able to talk all that you want, text whoever you want, and feel better knowing you are using your phone in a way that is safe.

3. Non smart phone- If the above two steps are too much of a "hassle" for you then the only other option you have is to replace your smart phone with a basic version that's only functions are to text and make phone calls. Although these devices still put off radio frequency radiation, they are far safer than any smart phone on the market. However, most of these types of phones are no longer available in stores and therefore must be purchased on websites such as eBay. If you are purchasing a new phone that claims to have a low SAR rating, remember that that has nothing to do with the radio frequency radiation levels. Therefore, make sure to check the phones exposure levels with your radio frequency meter. If they are high, return the phone and try again.

Interior remediation "Bluetooth devices"-

In most homes I have found that there are numerous Bluetooth devices ranging from speakers to wireless headphones to even air purifiers. Unfortunately, most of these devices do not have an option to turn the Bluetooth off. Therefore, the best bet is to get rid of anything that is Bluetooth and replace them with the safer wired version. I know that you may enjoy your music wirelessly using devices like air pods, but having wireless radio frequency radiation that close to your brain has side effects. Just go online, search wireless headphones and headaches, and read through the various complaints. By swapping out your wireless Bluetooth technology, you will eliminate another layer of radio frequency radiation within your home. However, that doesn't mean that you place them in a box and save them. While they are off, they still emit high levels of radio frequency radiation. If you are not interested in getting rid of your Bluetooth technology but are willing to try to see if you feel a difference, there is a solution. Get a box large enough to hold all of your Bluetooth devices, line the entire box with tinfoil, making sure that there are no cuts or rips in the foil, place your devices inside of the box and take additional measurements. If you sealed the box correctly, not even a turned-on Bluetooth device will penetrate through, leaving your meter reading at zero. Then place the box in a safe place, until the day you decide to get rid of them.

Interior remediation "Computers"-

Most of the homes that I complete inspections for have numerous laptop computers and tablets. Unfortunately, these are some of the most dangerous devices for radio frequencies inside of the home. Luckily, there is an easy solution to remediate these sources. For starters, just because the device is plugged into an ethernet cable, doesn't mean that it is safe. If the laptop you are using still has WiFi turned on, it is going to constantly be searching for a source to connect to and therefore sending out pulsed radio frequency signals. For this, all that you need to do is go into your laptop or desktop computers settings and disable to WiFi function. By doing this, the pulsed radio frequency signals will stop. Another source of high radio frequency pulsed signals coming from your laptop or desktop computer is from your Bluetooth connectivity. Even if you have nothing connected with Bluetooth, pulsed radio frequency signals will still continue to be sent until you disable them in your settings. So, in order to make sure that your laptop or desktop computer is safe to use, make sure that it is plugged into ethernet, the WiFi option is disabled, and the Bluetooth option is disabled as well. This is the only way to ensure that you are not blasting yourself with high levels of radio frequency radiation. On a side note, your laptop should also never be used on your lap. Although it is deceiving and states "lap" in the name, it was never actually intended to be used on your lap. However, there are "shields" that can be placed under your laptop if you are not willing to stop using your laptop on your lap. For those, look up defender shield products on Amazon. They are roughly $100 dollars and could block some of the radiation from your devices while being used on your lap (I do not recommend you using it on your lap.)

Interior remediation "smart appliances"-

Remediating your smart appliances and devices can be easy or hard. For example, if you come across an Alexa, Siri or google home device, you simply just follow the same remediation advice given for your Bluetooth devices and get rid of them. There are no devices like that that operate on ethernet connectivity. If you come across a smart appliance such as: smart refrigerator, smart microwave, or a smart washer/dryer, then remediating can be difficult. Most of these appliances do not have an option to switch off the WiFi capability and therefore you will remain surrounded by radio frequency radiation. The remediation recommendation that I give my clients is to get rid of any appliance that has "smart" in the title.

Return them, sell them, trade them in, just don't keep them. Although they may seem convenient, your health is ultimately more important.

Interior remediation "microwave"-

For the majority of the population, using a microwave is a major source used to "cook" food. However, as you learned during the inspection portion, microwaves put off a large amount of wireless radio frequency radiation. For remediation, simply do not use your microwave. Not only does it strip your food of its beneficial nutrients, but it blasts you with radio frequency radiation up to 30 feet away. If you are unable to cook without a microwave, I suggest purchasing a cook book and learning how to make meals on a gas stove top or in the oven. It may seem hard at first to give up your microwave, but in the end it will prove worth it.

After completing the radio frequency remediation portion of your home inspection, go back around the exterior and interior of the property and re check your work. Make sure that there are no other sources of radio frequencies on the property and that the meter reading remains as close to zero as possible. Once you have confirmed that the radio frequencies are as close to zero as possible, and the results of the remediation are documented in the remediation section of the inspection form, you are now ready to continue on with the inspection.

Steps 6 & 7-

Magnetic Field Inspection and Remediation

Growing up, my house was surrounded by high voltage powerlines. One of which was situated less than 20 feet from my bedroom window. At night I would fall asleep to the sound of electricity buzzing on the wires and thought it was the coolest thing. Twenty years later I learned that living that close to high voltage powerlines was actually not cool and extremely bad for your health. Not only was I living close to higher electrical fields, but I was also near a higher than normal magnetic field. When it comes to these types of fields there's not a whole lot that you can do in an affordable range to eliminate the problem. Therefore, the best thing you can do in a high magnetic field environment is move. It may seem drastic but you'll thank me in the long run.

Magnetic fields are created from the electrical current flowing along a metallic path. In order for the magnetic field to be generated, a source of electricity needs to be supplied. Without electricity flowing, the magnetic field disappears. For example, when you plug a lamp into a wall, with it off but still plugged in, an electric field exists in/surrounding the lamps cord. Once the lamp is switched on, electrical current flows and a magnetic field is created in/surrounding the lamps cord. The stronger the electrical current, the further out the magnetic field will extend. The higher the voltage, the stronger the electrical field will be.

Unlike the radio frequency recommended safe levels, the FCC has nothing to do with the magnetic field safety standards and therefore the standards are recommended by the IEEE (Institute of Electrical and Electronics Engineers). According to the IEEE, 9,040 mG is the highest exposure level allowable. Interestingly, Building Biologists disagree and state that 1 mG should be the highest safe exposure level. Below I have broken down the various safety standards and recommended standards in an easy to read format:

1. 9,040 mG = IEEE
2. 1 mG = Building Biologists

The most common sources of high magnetic fields can best be understood by breaking them down into two separate categories: Exterior and Interior. Although the list may be small, the dangers associated are large.

*Most common **exterior** sources*

1. High voltage powerlines
2. Breaker box
3. Solar panels

*Most common **interior** sources*

1. Faulty wiring
2. Motors
3. Transformers

At first glance, the list above may seem intimidating and somewhat confusing. I mean, how are you supposed to know if your home has faulty wiring? That is where this part of the guide comes in handy. By following the steps listed below you will learn how to properly inspect and remediate your home of high magnetic fields. So, if you live near a high voltage powerline, don't start packing your bags just yet. Instead, continue reading and you may learn that your home isn't as bad as you think—in regards to magnetic fields.

Most likely, you may have additional sources of magnetic fields as the list above is only the most common sources and not all of them. Therefore, by learning how to inspect and remediate the most common sources, you will hopefully be able to inspect and remediate any other sources of magnetic fields within your home. Below I have broken down what you will be doing during the magnetic field inspection portion of the EMF home inspection. The following 3 steps will be discussed in detail throughout the chapter:

Step 1- Establish Baseline
Step 2- Exterior of the property
Step 3- Interior of the property

Step 1- Establish Baseline

By now you should have done a walk-through of the exterior and interior of the property, and established a baseline measurement of the magnetic fields present. On the inspection form, the column labeled "baseline" should be completely filled out. If it is not completed, moving on to step 2 of the radio frequency inspection is not advised.

Step 2- Exterior of the property

Head outside to the exterior of the property, making sure to have your magnetic field meter (NFA 1000) in hand. This is where the type of meter you own makes a very big difference in the results of the inspection. If you are not using the meter recommended in the meter chapter (NFA 1000), the readings on your meter may not register due to the lack of sensitivity and therefore you may not have an accurate sense of the true magnetic field on your property.

With your magnetic field meter on, begin this portion of the inspection by walking around the front of the exterior of the house. Unlike the radio frequency meter, this meter requires you to walk a little slower due to the fact that the antenna is inside the device itself and not an exterior attachment. If you live in a house where there are above ground powerlines, walk towards the powerlines with your meter. However, you may want to walk towards the street anyways because in some states the powerlines are buried. If by chance they are buried, the magnetic field tends to extend upward from the ground approximately 3-6 feet directly above the source. If your home has above ground powerlines the magnetic field will more often than not exceed safe limits the closer you get to being underneath them.

Besides powerlines, I have only come across one other source of a high magnetic field on the front of a property. That source was from improper wiring of an external front porch light. With that in mind, you should be turning on and off the exterior lighting of the property in order to gain a true measurement of the magnetic field. For example, one of my clients was an avid "do it yourself" type of individual. Anything that needed to be done to his home, he did it himself rather than hiring a professional. When his wife asked him to install a light on the front porch area of his house, he did so with ease. A few weeks after installing the new light, his wife began getting extreme migraines whenever she would sit outside to read, underneath the light. Thinking that it could be the lightbulb itself, she had her husband replace the lightbulb for a "less bright one." After that didn't work to eliminate her migraines, she tried avoiding the area all together in order to "test" if it was really the light. To her surprise, as long as she avoided siting under the light, her migraines were nonexistent. Over the next few days she researched "migraines and lights" and came across an article on the dangers of EMFs. That is where I came in. After arriving at their home, it was discovered that her husband had wired the electrical component of the light incorrectly, leading to a higher than normal magnetic field whenever the light was switched on. Having an electrician fix the wiring solved the problem and eliminated the high magnetic field as well as the migraines she was experiencing while sitting under the light.

After walking around the front of the property and finding any sources of elevated magnetic fields, make sure to document your findings on your inspection form under the "inspection" column. Next head to the side of the house and continue searching with your magnetic field meter for any spikes in the readings. If you are on the side of the house where there is a breaker box, here is where you will most likely stop due to high readings. In general, magnetic fields will extend 3-6 feet from the source and dissipate the further away you get. Make a note on a scratch piece of paper as to where the breaker box is located. For example, is it located on the other side of a bedroom or is it on the side of your garage? Knowing where the breaker box is located will come in handy during the remediation phase of the inspection.

Next to the breaker panel box, you may notice an additional box or two if you have solar panels (pictured left). These boxes will put off the same high levels of magnetic fields as the breaker box itself. This is information you should already have from the pre inspection checklist but in some cases I have had individuals not know that their house had solar panels. Once you have completed the sides of the house, head to the backyard for the final portion of the exterior inspection of magnetic fields.

In most of the inspections I have conducted, the backyards are relatively low in regards to magnetic fields. However, if the individual has a pool the magnetic field near the pool pump/motor has been very high. For inspection purposes, I typically have the individual turn on the pool pump in order to gain a measurement of the magnetic field. Above ground jacuzzies have also been a major source of high magnetic fields.

If you are lucky enough to not have any above ground powerlines, an exterior breaker box, wiring problems, or a pool/above ground jacuzzi, then you may find that the magnetic field on the exterior of your property is zero. If you do however have any of the above-mentioned sources of high magnetic fields, remediation is necessary. Although you may want to start remediating the sources immediately, waiting until after you have inspected the interior of the home for high magnetic fields is advised. Prior to heading to the interior of the property, make sure you have documented any sources of high magnetic fields on the exterior of the property on the inspection form.

Step 3- Interior of the property

With your magnetic field meter in hand, walk through the interior of the property room by room, starting at room number 1. Walk through the room, pointing the meter at every wall, the ceiling and the floor, making sure to cover every inch. If the meter reading "spikes", follow the spiked reading until you find the source.

In room number 1 (family room in most homes), the most common sources of high magnetic fields are devices that are currently plugged into the wall. Check computer chargers, cell phone chargers, televisions, and even desktop computers. While inspecting the magnetic fields remember that the field itself typically extends 3-6 feet from the source. So, if the meter spikes, follow the readings until you find the actual source. From 6 feet away the meter measurement will more often than not be lower than if you were 5 inches from the source. Also, make sure to switch lights on and off to gain an accurate measurement. You may also want to turn devices on and off as well to measure the magnetic field strength when in use. For example, during a home inspection I came across a family room that didn't have any lights in their ceiling. Instead, they had floor and table lamps. During the day, the lamps were all unplugged so that the outlets could be used for their additional devices. At first, I went through the room and did an inspection, measuring the various devices and found a lot of common sources. Nothing out of the ordinary. Then as I was leaving the room, the client said "we don't usually have this many devices in here. At night we plug our lamps in." Since the lamps were stored inside their hall closet during the day, I had no idea that they were used. After plugging them in, the problem became evident. The lamps were extremely old, were ungrounded, and the wiring was exposed and faulty, creating a very high magnetic field inches from where they sat and watched television. After replacing the lamps with new ones, the problem was solved.

After completing room number 1 and documenting the various sources of magnetic fields, move to room number 2 (the kitchen in most homes). The kitchen is going to be where a majority of the high magnetic field problems will be. Walk around the room very slowly, making sure to cover every area. In most homes you will find that the largest source is the refrigerator, the dishwasher (when it is running) and then the electric stove (when turned on). Here is where turning on and off appliances is necessary. Remember that when there is no electricity running through the appliance, there is no magnetic field. So, what I have my clients do is take me through their routine in the kitchen. Questions I typically ask during this reenactment of their routine are: When do you run the dishwasher? How often are you using appliances like a blender, crock pot or an air fryer? Do you use your electric stove often? These types of questions help me to see which appliances they are using on a daily basis and therefore I am able to measure them. If you want to do a similar experiment as to the one done with radio frequencies in the previous chapter, then have the individual take out their blender. Plug the blender in, place the magnetic field meter 6 feet away and hit start. The meter will immediately spike to off the chart levels, over 6 feet away. That is when I say "I bet you stand right next to the blender while it is going, right?" Sadly, everyone says yes, and then follows it up with some sort of explanation as to them never being informed of the dangers.

Once you have completed room number 2 (the

kitchen) continue to inspect the rest of the home one room at a time. One of the more commonly missed appliances is the vacuum. If the home has carpet, chances are that they also have a vacuum. Make sure to plug the vacuum in, check the magnetic field when it is running, and document your findings.

Another commonly missed appliance is the hair dryer. When a hair dryer is plugged in and in use, it is held inches away from the head, with a very large magnetic field. One of my clients for example, is a hair dresser. She spends her entire day holding a hair dryer in her hand and has seen her health decline in correlation to when she started her job. For the rest of the population, hair dryers are typically in use for less than 20 minutes a day, tucked back into a drawer and easily missed during an inspection. So, make sure to go over all of the appliances the individual uses during the day when completing the magnetic field inspection. It may seem like a lot to do, but during the remediation it will prove helpful.

Once you get to the room where the breaker box is located on the other side of the wall (typically the garage), make sure to take extra time measuring the magnetic field readings. Find the spot on the wall where it is located. Press the meter against the wall and then start walking backwards from the source until the number gets to zero. If you have a tape measure with you, measure the distance. In most cases it will extend 3-6 feet from the wall. On a side note, make sure to do the same thing for the room where the refrigerator is located on the other side. This will be helpful during the remediation phase.

More recently, dimmer switches have become more and more popular in the homes that I have inspected. Unfortunately, they too are a large source of high magnetic fields. If your home has dimmer switches, make sure to test them with your magnetic field meter by turning them on and off.

After you have completed the entire interior of the property, located all of the sources of high magnetic fields, the next thing to do, prior to remediation is ensure that all of the inspection column on the inspection form is filled out. After making sure your documentation is in order, next you will be remediating the sources of the problem areas.

Remediation

Remediating high magnetic fields can be nearly impossible, but I've done it, and so can you. However, some of my clients have actually moved to another home because the source of the magnetic field (high voltage powerlines) couldn't be removed and were causing them health problems. In those extreme cases, the health of their family was more important than their house and upon moving their health significantly improved. A golden rule my fiancé came up with was "when in doubt, get out", and it applies greatly to magnetic fields. In other instances, simply replacing an old appliance could eliminate the problem. For example, one of my very first clients contacted me because he was having horrible headaches and believed it was because of radio frequencies coming off of his smart television. After inspecting his home, I discovered that his problem was not only due to excessive radio frequencies coming from his smart television, but mainly because of where his couch was situated. Since he worked from home, his couch was his office, and his couch just so happened to back up to his kitchen wall. Where he sat on the couch was exactly behind where his refrigerator was (2 feet away), and the magnetic field it put off was so high my meter couldn't read it. Each time the motor kicked on he would say "can you feel that?" And I would reply by showing him the meter and explaining what was happening. It turned out that the refrigerator motor was not in the best condition and had needed to be replaced for quite some time. So, he switched out his entire refrigerator and the magnetic field significantly decreased. We also rearranged his work area so that his back wasn't up against the wall where the refrigerator was. After that, no more headaches.

Below you will learn how to remediate the most common exterior and interior high magnetic fields that in most cases don't involve moving and without breaking the bank. Some of the techniques may seem extreme, and they may be, but trying them could make all the difference. As a reminder, I have included the most common sources of exterior and interior high magnetic field culprits below.

*Most common **exterior** sources*

1. High voltage powerlines
2. Breaker box
3. Solar panels

*Most common **interior** sources*

1. Faulty wiring
2. Motors
3. Transformers

Exterior remediation "high voltage powerlines"-

If your home has high voltage powerlines in a close enough proximity to cause high magnetic field readings, you have two options for remediation: Having the power lines buried, or moving to a new home. If the exterior of your property is not affected by high voltage power lines, you can skip this remediation step.

For those of you who own your home, the value of the property can be affected by the "curb appeal." Having powerlines littering the view of the house, has definitely proven to lower a home's value. By getting them buried, you will not only boost your curb appeal, but also lower the risk of health complaints from high magnetic fields. Some states will actually burry them for free, all you have to do is contact your utility company or city and ask. In most other cases, if you want them buried you are going to be stuck with the bill. Which can vary drastically in price. Some of my clients have called and gotten quotes for upwards of $25,000. If that is not an option and the magnetic field is high, the only other option for remediation is to move.

If you are moving to a new home, make sure to check antennasearch.com prior to going out to tour the home. Then, go onto google earth, click street view and look around the house to see if there are any above ground powerlines. This can also be a question you ask your realtor prior to visiting the location.

Exterior remediation "breaker box"-

Hopefully your breaker box is located on the exterior of your house. In most cases it is on the outside of the garage. If it is on the outside of your garage then avoiding that area is the only option for exterior remediation. If you have seating set up near it, move the seating area. On the interior of your garage, if you have a work station set up less than 6 feet from where the breaker box is located, move your work station. If that is not possible then you are left with only one other option for remediation: "mu metal". On the website LessEMF.com there is a sheet of metal called mu metal that actually shields against magnetic fields. Unfortunately, it is very pricey and therefore most people chose to move their work stations rather than make that sort of financial investment. If you do decide to purchase mu metal, it comes in a sheet, and is intended to be mounted on the wall behind where the breaker box is located. Instructions for installation are included and can be installed in a matter of minutes.

Interior remediation "faulty wiring"-

When you think of wiring within a home, the thought tends to be that if the lights work, the wiring is fine. However, that type of thinking can get you into trouble. On average, about 25% of the homes I conduct inspections for have wiring errors that are directly linked to high magnetic fields. For those of you who are not electricians or know wiring, I will explain what faulty wiring/wiring errors tend to look like. The easiest way to understand this concept is to look at the wiring a lamp comes with. Typically, it has two wires that are close together, forming the cord that you use to plug into the wall. One of the wires is called the "hot" and the other is the "neutral" wire, forming what is called an electrical circuit. With the wires together, the magnetic fields cancel each other out. If you were to split the wires down the center and separate them from each other, the field is no longer cancelled, leading to a high magnetic field in-between them. Now take that same analogy and think of the wiring within your walls. Sometimes the hot and the neutral wire are separated, causing a magnetic field that extends outward from the source and into your living space. This can be discovered upon switching on a light switch, supplying electricity to the light and then taking a reading with your magnetic field meter. The remediation for this is simple. Call an electrician and let them know that you have a wiring error within one (or more) of your walls. Most electricians are familiar with how to fix this problem and for a relatively cheap price. However, if the problem is not in your walls but on an appliance such as a lamp, replacing the lamp or getting a new cord installed with properly wired hot and neutral wires is recommended.

A good way to check and see if the problem truly is faulty wiring, is to head out to the breaker box and cut the power to the room where the supposed magnetic field source is located. If your meter readings were correct and there was a high magnetic field due to faulty wiring, the field will be eliminated by turning off the breaker to that room. Once the breaker is cut, remeasure the source in question. Hopefully that does the trick and eliminates the source. If not, continue flipping breakers on and off one at a time until you find the source. Then, until the electrician comes out to fix the problem, leave the breaker switched off so that you are not getting exposed to a high magnetic field while you wait. Remember to document what you are doing in order to keep track of which breakers you have already tested.

Interior remediation "motors"-

Anything in your home that has a motor in it and requires electricity to work, will have a magnetic field. However, not all of them will be high enough to cause concern. If for example you are inspecting a home and come across a blender, and you follow the recommended advice during the inspection process by turning it on to gain a measurement, you may not have a high reading. If that is the case, you are lucky. Unfortunately, most blenders today have large enough motors that the magnetic field extends outward and is unsafe to be around. The remediation for this would be to replace the device or if that is not an option, limit its use as much as possible. And if you are using it, press start and stand more than 10 feet away until it is complete. Distance is your friend with magnetic fields.

If you find that your work environment is near your refrigerator (within 10 feet), move your work environment to an area that is further away. For example, one of my clients lived in an apartment where the refrigerator of the apartment below her was located directly under where she slept. Its magnetic field radiated upward, through the floor, and into the area where her bed was located. In order to eliminate the magnetic field from radiating her all night while in bed, we moved her bed to a spare room. She eventually ended up moving into a house because she didn't like having to avoid her old room.

Another appliance that tends to have a very large magnetic field is a dryer. Having the client place a few items inside of the dryer and hit start will reveal that it is a very large source. For this remediation, the recommendation I give my clients is to try and avoid doing laundry while you are inside of your home and especially not at night while you are sleeping. If at all possible, start the dryer right before you leave for work or to run errands. That way, you are not directly being affected by the magnetic field present while the dryer is running. When the dryer is not in use, unplug it.

Interior remediation "transformers"-

Anything that has a transformer in your home will put off a high magnetic field. However, knowing if it is a transformer or a motor that is putting off the magnetic field may prove complicated. In some apartments that I have done inspections for, the breaker box is located on the inside of the master bedroom and has been called a "transformer box." If you find yourself in a situation where the breaker box/ transformer box is located on the interior of the house, the same options for the exterior of the house apply: stay away from it or cover it with mu metal. If it is in your master bedroom, make sure that it is as far away from where you sleep as possible. If that is not possible, then you may need to invest in mu metal. Fortunately, the website LessEMF.com provides a prefabricated picture frame option with mu metal lining the back. Once purchased, you simply put the picture frame over the panel and it eliminates or greatly reduces the magnetic field.

Interior remediation "chargers"-

A commonly missed portion of the magnetic field remediation is: chargers. If you have a computer, take a look at the charging cable. The cable will have some sort of box situated on it. That box creates a magnetic field that extends out 3-6 feet. And if you are like me, you leave your computer plugged in while in use, which means the charger is near your feet. In some cases, I used to find myself resting my foot on the box situated on the cable. Other chargers that have the same sort of box situated on the cable, also put off magnetic fields, some higher than others. For remediation, simply unplug any of the devices that you are not using. Especially near where you sleep. When they are in use, make sure that they are as far away from your body as possible. Remember, distance is your friend with magnetic fields.

After completing the magnetic field remediation portion of your home inspection, go back around the exterior and interior of the property and re check your work. You should also compare the baseline inspection measurements to the remediation measurements. Then, make sure that there are no other sources of magnetic fields on the property and that the meter reading remains as close to zero as possible. Once you have confirmed that the magnetic fields are as close to zero as possible, and the results of the remediation are documented in the remediation section of the inspection form, you are now ready to continue on with the inspection.

Steps 8 & 9-

Electric Field Inspection and Remediation

When I first started conducting home inspections for clients, the process took an extremely long time — mainly because of this step. Checking the electrical fields can be particularly time consuming if you don't know what to look for and if you are using an electric field meter. If you are using an electric field meter, this part of the process could add hours onto your inspection. However, I am not saying that you can skip this step. What I am saying is that there is a smarter, faster and more efficient way to get the job done. Like the old saying goes, "work smarter, not harder."

Rather than beginning this portion of the inspection with an electric field meter, I use my body as a meter with a device that I call "The Body Voltage Meter." Using this meter, I am able to determine the source of the electrical field problem faster than if I were to use any other meter. This is simply because the meter itself measures how much electricity is flowing through your body at any given time (a number which should always be 0). Once the source is discovered, I then use an electrical field meter to pinpoint the exact location and double check my work. For example, recently I completed a home inspection for a client that was complaining of not being able to sleep because she felt "jittery and vibratey." She also suffered from headaches, but only in the evening time. With my body voltage meter in hand I had her walk me through her evening routine. We walked around her kitchen, flipped on lights, pretended to do laundry, and then went into her bedroom. The meter itself stayed relatively low until we stepped foot into her bedroom. This is where she said her headaches began, and the meter proved why. Standing on her bedroom floor with her shoes off, she had 4.5 volts (4,500mV) of electricity flowing through her body. When I saw this reading my eyes lit up, but not as much as they did next. I then had her lay on her bed as if she were going to sleep and had her hold the body voltage meter herself. We then turned on her side table lamp, overhead fan, and television in order to mimic her nighttime environment. The meter read 8 volts (8,000mV) of electricity flowing through her body. We were both shocked, pun intended. She then asked "is that why I feel vibratey at night?" I replied "Yes! Your body is vibrating because it is in a constant state of excitement due to the amount of electricity flowing through your body, opening your voltage gated calcium channels and flooding your cells with excess calcium." With a look of understanding she then asked "what does that mean for me?" I then said "If we get that number to drop below 100mV, I can almost guarantee that you will sleep better tonight." After discovering that the source was coming from her walls, I used my electric field meter to confirm my findings and then proceeded to mitigate the problem. We were able to drop her body voltage in bed from 8 volts (8,000mV) to 85mV by making a few improvements, and that night she slept better than she had in years. In fact, a week later she contacted me to let me know that she no longer felt "jittery or vibratey" and that she hadn't had a headache or trouble sleeping since I fixed the problem. As you can see, I worked smarter and not harder to eliminate the problem by using my body voltage meter. Within this chapter you will not only learn how to measure electric fields using an electric field meter, but also use the body voltage meter you created from the chapter on meters.

What is an electric field? An electric field is simply the voltage from one point to another. On average an electric field can extend up to 8 feet from a source. Which means that when you plug a lamp into a wall, electricity powers the lamp, and a measurable electric field extends outward from the lamp up to 8 feet away. Even without anything plugged into the wall, the wiring inside of the wall (unless turned off at the breaker) will create an electric field that extends outward and into your home. For an example of what an electric field is capable of, go to youtube.com and type in "lightbulbs in ground light up" and watch what happens. In short, an individual places multiple lightbulbs in the ground under a powerline. They are not connected to any batteries or power source. However, there is a large enough electric field created from the stray volage coming off of the powerlines that all of the lightbulbs light up.

Most people would agree that electricity is dangerous and that touching any "live electric wire" could be potentially catastrophic. However, most individuals do not know that electric fields are just as dangerous. Along with Magnetic Fields, the IEEE also recommends the safety standards for electric fields. Their recommended highest safe exposure levels are 10,000 V/m. Building Biologists once again disagree and state their recommended highest safe exposure levels at 1.5 V/m. Below I have broken down the various safety standards and recommended standards in an easy to read format:

1. 10,000 V/m = IEEE
2. 1.5 V/m = Building Biologists

Another area that is affected through high electric fields is body voltage. Around any source of electricity, your body acts as an antenna and picks up the stray electricity. With the heart, brain, and many other organs within the human body operating on various electrical wavelengths, any excess electricity flowing through your body may cause adverse effects. Therefore, keeping your body away from electrical sources that may raise your body voltage is advised. As an expert on the matter, I advise my clients to try and keep their body voltage below 100 millivolts (mV) in order to allow optimal healing to occur. This however, can be extremely difficult to maintain due to everchanging environmental factors. Below I have listed my expert recommendation for ideal body voltage throughout the day and night:

1. 100mV or lower during the day.
2. 0mV at night.

The most common sources of high electric fields can best be understood by breaking them down into two separate categories: Exterior and Interior.

*Most common **exterior** sources*

1. High voltage powerlines
2. Stray ground current

*Most common **interior** sources*

1. Faulty wiring
2. Ungrounded 2-prong electronics
3. Power strips
4. Stray current on water pipes

You may notice that some of the most common sources of high electric fields are similar to the common magnetic fields. This is why establishing a baseline is so important to accomplish prior to the actual inspection. Anything that was remediated during the magnetic field remediation may directly impact the readings of the electric field and therefore changing your initial baseline measurements. However, that may not always be the case. That is why documentation is essential to an effective home inspection. Throughout this portion of the guide you will learn just how easy inspecting and remediating electric fields can be.

Most likely, you may have additional sources of electric fields as the list above is only the most common sources and not all of them. Therefore, by learning how to inspect and remediate the most common sources, you will hopefully be able to inspect and remediate any other sources of electric fields within your home. Below I have broken down what you will be doing during the electric field inspection portion of the EMF home inspection. The following 3 steps will be discussed in detail throughout the chapter:

Step 1- Establish Baseline
Step 2- Exterior of the property
Step 3- Interior of the property

Step 1- Establish Baseline

As you have seen by now, establishing a baseline is crucial to the success of the remediation. So, if you haven't completed the baseline of the electric fields within your home by now, your measurements may be different than if you were to have completed them first. By remediating radio frequencies and magnetic fields, the electric fields could inadvertently be affected and therefore the baseline skewed. That is why establishing a baseline should be done prior to the inspection and remediation process. If you haven't done a baseline measurement of the electric field, it isn't too late. Go back to the establishing a baseline chapter and complete the baseline readings for electrical fields now, if not completed on your documentation.

Step 2- Exterior of the property

For this step, two meters will be required. First you will be using the body voltage meter you created, and second you will use the electric field meter. This is where a partner is good to have (they can carry the second meter for you so that your hands are free to use the body voltage meter first). Begin at the front of the house by placing the grounding rod into the ground and attaching it to the body voltage meter. Remember, the meter must be grounded properly in order to establish an accurate reading. Then switch the meter on and carry it in one hand while the metal handle is attached and in your other hand.

Unlike the radio frequency meter where you could freely walk around the property, or the magnetic field meter where you walked a little slower, with the body voltage meter you are more restricted. First of all, you are tethered to the grounding rod which limits your mobility by having to move it to a new location every time you run out of slack. Secondly, in order to gain an accurate reading, you can't move at all. This is because walking creates static electricity and therefore interferes with the body voltage reading. By using the body voltage meter, you are essentially turning your body into an antenna in order to read how much electricity is flowing through you. The higher the reading, the higher the electrical field will be.

With your meter in hand and a firm grasp on the handle, begin by taking one step at a time around the front of the property. With each step, take a look at the meter to see what the current body voltage is. This step can take quite a long time with larger properties. If there are above ground powerlines walk over to them and take measurements, making sure to document your findings. On most occasions I tend to focus on the areas of the exterior of the property where the client spends most of their time. For example, in the front of the house some clients have been fortunate enough to have large front porches where seating areas are set up. I like to test these areas first by sitting where they sit and measuring the body voltage. That way I am aware of the areas that may need more attention. If the body voltage meter is above 100mV I then use the electric field meter to pin point the exact location of the problem. Some people may choose not to use the body voltage meter on the exterior of the house because it takes more time, at first. However, once you get the hang of it you will see that using the body voltage meter is not only easier but faster for measuring electric fields.

In the front of the house the typical high electric fields that you will run into are from powerlines (above ground or buried), from faulty wiring on exterior lighting or appliances, and stray voltage that is present in the soil (U.S. only). Unfortunately, the U.S. is the only country that I know of that chose the ground as a return path for electricity, rather than a return cable. This has then, in effect, electrified the soil that we stand on. This will result in you noticing that although there are no electrical sources around you, your body voltage may not be zero while standing outside.

After completing the front of the house, you will next remove the grounding rod and relocate it to the side of the house and continue the inspection. On the side of the house you will most likely run into high electric fields from the breaker box and from stray voltage on the water pipes running into the house. For example, while walking around the perimeter of a client's home

I noticed my body voltage spike from 30mV to 2,000mV (2 volts) when I passed near a certain area near the garage. Not knowing what caused my body voltage to spike, I slowly inspected the area until I found where the water pipe enters the house. Standing next to the water pipe my body voltage jumped even higher to 8,000mV (8 volts). Eventually, I determined that the source was the water pipe itself by taking out my electric field meter and pinpointing its exact location. What that meant was that the stray voltage in the soil surrounding the house was attracted to the metal piping buried in the dirt, resulting in stray voltage being carried inside of the house through the piping. Don't worry if this is what is occurring at your home, as it is one of the most common sources of high electric fields on the properties I have inspected and is easily remediated.

Once the sides of the house are completed and documented under the inspection portion of the inspection form, head to the backyard for the final step of the exterior electric field inspection. In most of the backyards I have inspected, the main sources of high electric fields come from faulty wiring on exterior lighting, pool equipment, and stray current from the ground being amplified on metal chairs. However, in one extreme case there was a variable that I was unaware of until witnessing it myself. In this example, my client contacted me because she was experiencing headaches and brain fog in the evening time. So, I began my inspection of her home later in the day than I usually would, knowing that the source of the problem could be related to the lighting she uses when it is dark outside. After completing my baseline measurements, everything seemed like a normal home inspection. That was until the sun set. As soon as I made my way into the backyard for the inspection, I noticed that the body voltage meter was reading levels 100x higher than they were during the baseline inspection. This was something that I had never seen before. Usually, they will remain around the same until remediation occurs, then the numbers go down. However, something was different at this house. In the distance, I noticed a high school about a mile away with large stadium lights that were so bright that I couldn't stare directly at them without being blinded. The client informed me that these lights went on every Friday, Saturday, and Sunday during various sport seasons. With that information in hand, I completed the inspection and as much of the remediation that I could and then scheduled to come out to her house on a night that the lights wouldn't be on in order to retake the measurements. Sure enough, on the night that I came back out to reinspect the backyard, the lights were off and the body voltage was below 100mV. For the next few weeks I loaned her my body voltage meter and had her take measurements of her backyard during specific times in order to truly determine if the lighting from over a mile away was impacting the electric field on the exterior of her home. To my surprise, every night that the stadium lights were on, the body voltage meter would read over 10,000mV (10 volts). On the nights that the stadium lights were not on, the body voltage meter would read under 100mV. After that I decided to take matters even further and attempt to inspect her home on a night where the stadium lights would come on and wait for them to turn off. The entire time the lights were on, the meter read over 10,000mV, then at exactly 10:00pm, the stadium lights turned off and the meter dropped to below 100mV. Although this was a rare case, it just goes to show you that there are many external factors that may impact your homes electric field and therefore measurements must be taken during various times of the day. After discovering this variable, I began testing homes in the evening time as well in order to account for things that are not on during the day, such as: street lights, neighbors exterior lighting, holiday lights, and stadium lighting.

In another example, I had one client with solar panels where the results were the exact opposite. During the day the body voltage was extremely high due to excess electricity being produced from the panels. At night the panels would turn off and the body voltage would drop to below 100mV. This was discovered by turning the exterior lighting on during the day, testing the electric field using the body voltage meter, and then testing the same exterior lighting at night when the panels were off. If testing at night is not possible, then at a minimum make sure to test the electric field with the exterior lighting on and off. If the numbers change drastically, remediation may be necessary.

Checking the seating areas in the backyard is an area that must be thoroughly checked as well. With your body voltage meter in hand, sit down on the chairs that the client has set up in the backyard. Chances are, they are made out of metal with a cushion situated on the seat. As you will notice, if there is metal in the chair, the body voltage will be higher. This is because similar to electricity being attracted to the body, it is also attracted to metal.

Once the exterior of the property has been thoroughly inspected using the body voltage meter to locate the vicinity of the electric field and the electric field meter to pinpoint the exact source, make sure to document your findings. At this point, do not begin the exterior remediation until after you inspect the interior of the property. Prior to heading to the interior of the property, make sure that any sources of high electric fields are documented on the inspection form.

Step 3- Interior of the property

When you walk into the interior of the home, make sure that you disconnect the grounding rod from the grounding cable, as you will not need it. Then, locate an outlet that you will be plugging your grounding cable into and test it with the ground receptacle tester in order to ensure that the outlet is properly grounded. Once you have determined that the outlet is properly grounded, plug the grounding cable into the ground portion of the outlet and begin walking around room number 1. Remember though, you must take a step, check the meter, take another step, check the meter, and so on. Simply walking throughout the room will generate static electricity (especially if there is carpet) and the reading on the meter will be inaccurate. So, make sure you are stopping and standing still while measuring the electric field with the body voltage meter.

In room number 1 (the family room in most houses) the areas that I like to start with are the seating areas. Sit on the couch, the chairs, the recliners, and take measurements of the body voltage. If there is carpet in the room, you will notice that the body voltage will be higher. This is because of static electricity generated by the carpet and your feet. You may know what I am referring to if you have ever "shocked" yourself on a doorknob while walking in socks on a carpeted floor. If not, feel free to do a little experiment and take your shoes off but keep your socks on. With your body voltage meter in hand, drag your feet on the carpet and watch the measurement go up drastically. Static electricity is also a warning you will see next to gas station pumps. The warnings recommend that you touch a metal part of your car in order to discharge your static electricity prior to touching the pump in order to avoid a "spark" which could ignite the gasoline.

After sitting in all of the seating areas, next you will want to stand near each of the walls in the room and take measurements with the lights both on and off. If the body voltage readings are low (under 100mV) with the lights off but then are high with the lights on (over 100mV), you may have a faulty wiring problem. However, it could also be the type of lightbulb that you are using. Some light bulbs save energy by turning off thousands of times per second, generating high electric fields as well as dirty electricity.

In each of the rooms make sure that you are turning on and off any of the devices or appliances that are inside of the room, making sure to note changes in body voltage in the on or off position. If the room has a lamp, stand near the lamp and turn it on. You will notice the body voltage go up immediately, especially if it is not grounded. Basically, any device or appliance that is not grounded will generate a higher electric field than if it were grounded. The way that you can tell if a device is grounded is if it has 3 prongs coming off of the plug. If there are only 2 prongs, then the device is not grounded and therefore a problem for electric fields. This is because if the device were grounded then any stray electricity is safely discharged through the ground port on the outlet rather than generating a higher electric field that extends 6-8 feet from the source. Electricity is smart. It wants to ground itself, and looks for the path of least resistance in order to do so. In most cases if the appliance is grounded then the path of least resistance is the ground port on your outlet. If it is not grounded then the electricity looks for another path to ground itself and typically will find an alternative source such as a piece of metal or our bodies. This is because our bodies contain large amounts of water and attract stray electricity like an antenna.

The next room you will come across with high electric fields will be in room number 2, which in most homes is the kitchen. Remember to unplug the body voltage meter from the outlet and relocate it prior to moving rooms. If there is a kitchen island situated in the middle of the room, I like to sit at it first and take measurements. More often than not, by placing your arms on the granite or marble counter top, you will notice that the body voltage meter reading will skyrocket. This is because the stray electricity is attracted to the granite and marble counter tops, transferring to your body when touched. Along with the counter tops, touch anything and everything inside of the kitchen that you would typically touch on a daily basis and take measurements. You will notice the highest electric field being generated from ungrounded devices and especially an electric stove top. Document anything and everything that exceeds safe limits.

After completing room number 2 (the kitchen), make your way to the next room and continue turning on lights, sitting in chairs, turning on devices and appliances, and touching everything that you use on a daily basis, while documenting your measurements. When you get to a bathroom, there are two areas of high electric fields that I typically see: the ventilation fan, and the faucets. The ventilation fan when in the on position generates a high electric field and therefore causes the body voltage to exceed safe limits. This is due to the motor inside of the fan and not the fan itself.

The most common bathroom high electric field comes from the faucets. This is due to the stray electricity from the exterior of the house being attracted to the metal water pipes and making its way inside. For example, one of my clients contacted me about feeling "jittery" at night and thought that it had to do with his neighbors WiFi. After inspecting his home, it was determined that the source of the problem was not his neighbors WiFi, but stray current on his water wipes. When I pointed this out to him, he replied "is that why I shock myself sometimes when I am turning the water on to brush my teeth?" After remediating the problem, he no longer shocked himself at night and no longer felt jittery. You would be surprised at how many people shock themselves on various metal devices in their homes on a daily basis and think that its normal.

When you get to the bedrooms, here is where you

must spend extra time measuring with the body voltage meter. Go around the room, sitting in any of the seating areas, flipping the lights on and off, overhead fans on and off, and touching any of the devices or appliances used on a daily basis. Then, when you get to the bed, lay on it. The body voltage on the bed should be below 100mV but in most of the homes that I visit, it is a lot worse than that, sometimes exceeding the limitations of my meter. The reason why it is so crucial to check the body voltage while in bed, is because the bed is where you spend a good portion of your day (hopefully 8 hours while sleeping). If you have electricity flowing through your body at night, your quality of sleep will be hindered, therefore resulting in an inability to heal. Knowing what your body voltage is in bed is a question that everyone should have an answer for. In the remediation portion you will learn just how big of a difference lowering the body voltage in bed will make towards your quality of sleep.

In some cases, I have had clients that had areas of their house that are not considered rooms, but have desks set up against the walls. In those homes I add an extra column and label it accordingly on the inspection form. Being as thorough as possible during the inspection will help make the remediation go as fast as possible. Make sure that after completing the interior portion of the inspection, all of the results have been documented, as well as the areas that need to be remediated.

Remediation

Remediating high electric fields and body voltage is

by far my favorite. Seeing the faces of my clients when I explain to them that they are sleeping in a sea of electricity and then fixing it, makes me feel like a magician. On numerous occasions I have helped individuals go from sleeping a few hours a night to sleeping uninterrupted for 8+ hours, all by "calming their sea of electricity." One particular example of an extremely successful remediation stands out more than others, mainly because this client was an electrician. For 22 years, he was a full-time electrician, servicing thousands of individuals electricity needs. To him, the thought of measuring one's body voltage was a foreign concept and something he struggled to accept as being his problem. He knew of the dangers of EMFs, which is why he contacted me, but the thought of stray electricity being attracted to his body made him angry to even discuss. During the inspection he followed me like a hawk, explaining how his problem isn't electricity related because "if it were then he would know." When it came to the part of the inspection where I was measuring the electric fields using my body voltage meter, his anger grew: "I wired this house myself, nothing is wrong with it, it's up to code, trust me." Then I showed him the ability to measure the A/C electric fields by turning the body into an antenna through the use of a body voltage meter. He was intrigued. After each high reading, he would say something along the lines of "well, turn the light off and it will go down" or "you aren't supposed to touch the wall with your hand, that's why it's high." His excuses were among some of the best that I have ever received.

When I remediated the electric field issue within his bedroom, lowering the body voltage from over

3,000mV to under 100mV, he was extremely skeptical that it would help. I said to him "give it a try and if it doesn't work for you, I will come out and return everything to the way it was before, and I will give you a full refund." I'll never forget the message I received from him that next morning: "OMG! I slept like a log! That was the best sleep of my life! I think you are onto something here with the whole body voltage thing. I will let you know in a week what I think." A week later he contacted me and said "I feel amazing! Every single night I have gotten better and better sleep. I have more energy during the day now and don't have to drink multiple cups of coffee to keep me going." As you can see, electrical fields affect everyone, electricians included. Below you will learn how to remediate the most common sources of electrical fields on the exterior and interior of your home. As a reminder, the most common sources are listed here:

*Most common **exterior** sources*

1. High voltage powerlines
2. Stray ground current

*Most common **interior** sources*

1. Faulty wiring
2. Ungrounded 2-prong electronics
3. Power strips
4. Stray current on water pipes

Exterior remediation "high voltage powerlines"-

There is a difference between high voltage powerlines

and regular powerlines. High voltage powerlines will more often than not, have a large white cylinder situated at the top of the pole. Towards the bottom there will also be a sign that says "Danger: High Voltage." If you have a high voltage powerline in close proximity to your home, and have measured the associated electrical fields, remediation may be necessary if the field is higher than optimal safe levels.

If you have an ordinary powerline, that doesn't say high voltage on it, chances are that it will not put off as high of an electric field as a high voltage powerline. However, most experts would agree that living near any sort of powerline is not advised and could pose health risks later on down the road. If you are following the precautionary principle of avoiding anything that may cause health problems, then remediation by burying the lines is recommended. This can be accomplished by following the same remediation methods found in the magnetic field section, under high voltage powerlines.

Exterior remediation "stray ground current"-

Due to the fact that the utility companies in the United States use the ground as a return path, the soil around most homes is electrified. This can be more or less intense depending on where your house is located on the power grid as well as how close you live to a power substation. A substation looks like an area where a bunch of powerlines are together, high voltage and regular voltage, all in close proximity, and typically fenced off with a sign that says "DANGER: STAY BACK, HIGH VOLTAGE". For example, one of my clients was staying at a hotel recommended by her doctor while she was receiving treatment for Lyme Disease. Across the street from this hotel was a substation and two large cell towers, less than 200 feet from her room. Walking around the exterior of the hotel, the body voltage meter was so high that my meter could not read it. The interior of the property was also so high that my meter could not read it. Which meant that the body voltage levels were over 24,000 mV or 24 Volts. This was not an environment someone looking to heal should have been in. The environment was this way due to the substation located across the street. The amount of electricity coming in and going out from this station caused the area surrounding it to become more electrified than a normal neighborhood would be and is a rarer situation. If you live near a power substation (see example below), chances are that your ground will have more stray voltage than if you didn't live near one.

Therefore, I recommend that people plan on moving if that is the case. It may seem extreme, but if your home is surrounded by high electrical fields from powerlines, substations and other various factors, you may find yourself facing health related problems down the road. What I tell my clients to do if they just so happened to be in a similar situation, is to "try it before you buy it." What that means is that I have them contact a friend or family member who doesn't live near a substation (or high voltage powerline), and have them stay with them for a week or so. Most of the time, the people who are living in high electric fields, are unaware of the problems that are associated with that environment until getting completely out. Once out they are able to recognize that previous areas of concern are no longer present and the association is therefore revealed. After they spend a week outside of their high electric field home environment, I have them return back to the house and spend the night. On every single occasion, my clients will feel the difference and choose to move to a better environment on their own. If moving is not an option and remediation of the exterior high electric field is not possible due to proximity to substations or high voltage powerlines, then prudent avoidance is the only recommendation.

Although "stray current on waterpipes" is an interior problem, remediating it requires making changes on the exterior of the property. On some occasions, the stray ground current from the exterior of the property is attracted to the metal waterpipes. This leads to stray current making its way into the interior of the property. Remediating this problem is simple and will result in a lower electric field within the home.

First, locate where the water pipe enters the home. Typically, this is located on the exterior of the property closest to the street but can be situated on the side of the garage under the breaker box or smart meter. Once located, make sure that your readings of the electric field are related to the piping and not some other hidden source. Then, contact a plumber and inform them that you want to "replace a small section of the metal pipe on the exterior of your house with PVC." Most plumbers will be confused and say "why would you want to do that?" Explaining to them that there is stray current on your pipes and by replacing a section on the exterior of your house with PVC it will eliminate the electric field from continuing along the metal path and into your home, may be necessary. This simple remediation solution for stray current on your waterpipes will eliminate the electric field on the interior of the house immediately upon installation but should be checked again with the electric field meter after completion. All together with labor, this remediation step has never cost more than a few hundred dollars and is usually completed in less than an hour with a certified plumbing expert.

Interior remediation "faulty wiring"-

In most of the homes that I have inspected, faulty wiring has been a major issue. Therefore, remediation will require more time on your behalf. The most common wiring issue that I have seen is in newer built homes as well as any home that has been remodeled. In newer built homes, corners are cut in order to lower costs, which results in faulty wiring. Although these homes are "up to code" in regards to basic electrical standards, electrical fields tend to be an area that is not tested by electricians. And as a homeowner, your only test seems to be that if the light turns on when you flip the switch, everything must be okay. I am here to tell you that that isn't always the case. If you are in a home where your body voltage goes up drastically when turning on a certain light switch, but does not in any other room, chances are that you have a wiring issue related to that specific switch. That being said, in most of the homes that I have inspected, there seems to be a trend of one or two rooms where the switches are wired incorrectly, creating a high electric field whenever the light is switched on. If that is the case, do not try to remediate the problem yourself. Contact a professional electrician and inform them of the problem. The script that I tell most of my "do it yourself" clients to say is "one of the light switches in my house is acting up and needs to be fixed. Can you come out and take a look?" Once the electrician is on your property, show them the electric field meter as well as the body voltage meter and then walk them through the results of the inspection. If you are working with a professional, they will more often than not be extremely interested in how you were able to discover that there was a wiring issue and then work with you to solve the problem. On most occasions the issue is simple and is remediated by fixing a few wires attached at the switch or at the actual fixture. Once it is fixed, retest again and feel free to show the electrician that the problem has been remediated.

If your electric field being high is not related to a specific switch being turned on or off, there are two other remediation steps you can take prior to contacting an electrician. First, note what your body voltage is within the room or area that is of concern. Then head out to your breaker box and flip the breaker off that is connected to that room, making sure to also document which breaker was switched off on your scratch piece of paper. Next head back inside and remeasure your body voltage in the room where the breaker is turned off. If the wiring problem is associated with that room, the body voltage meter reading should go down significantly. If it did not go down, then the problem is most likely not related to that room. Here is where it can get tricky, so make sure to follow these next steps carefully.

Next you will head back out to the breaker box, flip the breaker that you turned off back on, and then flip the entire system off by turning off the main breaker switch (usually this switch is located at the top of the other breakers, centered, and labeled "main breaker". This will cut all of the power to the inside of your home, so make sure that if you have any alarm systems or smoke detectors that are attached to the electricity in your home that you contact your alarm system company prior to this step. If your smoke detectors are wired into your home, they may turn back on in "test mode". Once all of the power is cut to your house, head back inside and into the room that is in question. Here is where you will take an additional measurement of your body voltage using the body voltage meter. This number should now be close to zero as you no longer have electricity within your home. If the number is not close to zero, and is above 100mV, your problem is exterior and therefore remediation may not be possible. If the number is close to zero, document it and head back out to the breaker box. The documented results should look something like this:

All breakers ON: 1,500mV
Bedroom 1 breaker OFF: 1,300mV
All breakers OFF: 0mV

Next, turn the main breaker back on. Once it is back on, go back inside and remeasure the body voltage within the room in question. In some cases, simply switching the power off and then on again has lowered the body voltage, therefore checking again prior to the next step is recommended. Once you have remeasured the room in question, head back outside and flip the breaker associated with that room back off again. Then, head back inside and remeasure the room, just to make sure the documented measurements are still the same. After that, head back outside to the breaker box and switch off the breaker that is associated with the room *next to* the room in question. For example: If the room in question is a bedroom and there is a bathroom next to that room, you will be turning off the breaker associated with that bathroom. Make sure to document which breakers you have turned off. By now there should only be 2 breakers turned off — the breaker to the room in question, and the breaker to the room next to it. After you have verified that both of the breakers are off, head back inside and take an additional measurement of the room in question. Your documented results should look something like this:

All breakers ON: 1,500mV
Bedroom 1 breaker OFF: 1,300mV
All breakers OFF: 0mV
Bathroom 1 breaker OFF: 0mV

If you notice that the body voltage is now at zero or as close to zero as possible, then you may have found the source of the faulty wiring. If the body voltage measurement did not go down, then head back out to the breaker box and turn off an additional breaker associated with another room near the room in question. In some homes the wiring problem is located in the kitchen, and by turning off the kitchen breaker, the room in question returns to a zero body voltage environment. So, by turning off the breakers one at a time and then checking your body voltage, you are essentially looking for the source of the faulty wiring.

Once you have a measured body voltage level that is as close to zero as possible, head back out to the breaker box and turn back on all of the breakers, except for the one that created the high body voltage reading. By following the example listed above, what that would look like is: turn back on the breaker to bedroom 1 and keep the breaker associated with bathroom 1 off. Then head back into the house and remeasure bedroom 1 (or the room in question). Your body voltage reading should still be as close to zero as possible if the problem truly was the room next to it. In homes that are multiple stories, if you have eliminated all of the breakers on one floor and the problem still remains, begin by switching off the breaker to the room located underneath the room in question.

After discovering which room has the faulty wiring by turning on and off the breakers, next you will head back outside and turn the breaker back on to that room. Then you will inspect the room further by turning on and off the various appliances or light switches within that room, trying to locate the source of the problem. If you turn the light switch on and your body voltage remains the same, move on to the fan. If the fan is on and the body voltage remains the same, move on to anything that is plugged into the wall. Unplug each of the devices or appliances that are plugged into the wall, head back into the room in question and remeasure the body voltage. For example, while completing this portion of the remediation for one of my clients, I discovered that the problem wasn't faulty wiring, but the dryer located in the garage. By unplugging the dryer inside of the garage, the client's bedroom located on the other side of garage read zero on the body voltage meter. Since the client was not in a financial position to purchase a new dryer, he decided on keeping it unplugged while it was not in use. By doing so, his body voltage in his bedroom remains at zero. Whenever he wants to dry his clothes, he plugs his dryer back in and avoids his bedroom until the cycle is complete.

It is always a good idea to unplug any of the devices that are not in use. Make it a habit to unplug your toaster, coffee pot, blow dryer, cell phone charger, television, and anything else that you do not need plugged in. It will not only lower your body voltage within your home, but will also lower your electricity bill. If you cannot locate the source of the high body voltage problem by turning off the breakers, flipping on and off switches, or unplugging devices and appliances, the problem is most likely the wiring within the walls. This can be remediated with the help of a professional electrician and should not be attempted by an amateur. If that is your case, contact a professional electrician and explain to them that you believe that you have a wiring problem in a specific room. Once they are on your property, walk them through what you have done to discover where the electrical wiring problem is located. The electrician will then be able to pinpoint the exact location of the problem, which in most cases is due to something inside of the wall being wired incorrectly. For this to be remediated, the electrician may need to open up the wall to fix the wiring problem, which can be costly.

Most of my clients however, choose to keep the breakers off to their bedrooms in order to remain in a zero body voltage environment while sleeping. Some clients even keep breakers off to the rooms that they do not use electricity that often in order to cut down on body voltage levels as well as their electrical bills. Although this may sound drastic, sleeping in a room with zero electricity flowing through the walls will result in deeper, more healing sleep. I personally sleep with zero electricity in my bedroom and use soy wax candles to light the room if necessary. The results are so amazing that a company actually invented a product called a "kill switch". The product is remote controlled and is attached to your breaker box by an electrician. At night or whenever you want the power cut to that room, you press the remote and the power turns off. This eliminates the need for you to go out to your breaker box and turn off the breaker to your room at night. However, if you are not interested in spending $400.00 on a kill switch, keeping the breakers off to the rooms that do not need electricity is recommended — if not all the time, then at least at night while you are sleeping.

Interior remediation "bedroom"-

Although the bedroom is not a common *source* of electrical field problems, it is however an area of the home that contains a large amount of easily remediated electrical fields. If during the electrical field inspection you come across high body voltage within the bedroom, remediation could make all the difference. Fortunately, this can be accomplished with a few easy steps that does not have to include turning the breaker box off in order to get a good night's sleep. The first step that I take when remediating a bedroom of high electric fields, is I unplug everything. In most bedrooms that I have inspected, there are side lamps, an alarm clock, a smart television, cell phone charger, a cable box, floor fan, and an Alexa. If any of those items are inside of the bedroom, I unplug all of them and have the client place them in a room that is not being used (i.e. the garage). Then I remeasure the body voltage everywhere inside of the room. In most cases, the body voltage will lower a significant amount just by eliminating anything that is plugged in. This is mainly because most of these devices are "ungrounded" (2 prongs vs. 3 prongs) and therefore create unnecessary high electric fields. If the devices are grounded, unplugging them will only slightly make a difference in the electric fields present. Some clients have been hesitant to get rid of their lamps, claiming that they will not be able to see at night without them. If that is the case, I place "puck lights" on their night stands as a replacement form of light. Puck lights are cheap and are battery operated making them safer than devices that plug into the wall. If an alarm clock is needed, I swap out the corded one for a battery operated one. However, if you are purchasing a battery-operated alarm clock, make sure that it is the most basic one possible and avoid ones with Bluetooth or WiFi capabilities.

Once everything is unplugged and devices are swapped for safer alternatives, I then inspect the bed. If the bedframe is made out of metal, the box spring has metal springs, or the mattress has metal in it, then remediation is possible. Metal as you already know, acts as an antenna for electric fields, which means that the metal inside of a bed could result in higher electric fields. Remediating this can be accomplished two ways: first, by swapping out the bedframe, box spring, or metal lined mattress for ones that do not contain any metal, or two, by grounding the metal. Swapping out anything in your bed that is metal for nonmetal versions is typically preferred. If you have a metal bedframe, a wooden one is a good alternative. If you have a metal box spring, there are ones that only contain wood. If your mattress has metal springs in it, there are numerous alternatives like memory foam, that do not have any metal. However, if replacing your metal bed is not financially possible, the other option is to ground the metal. This is accomplished by using something called a "grounding cable", available on Amazon for $20.00. Below I have outlined how to properly ground your bed using a grounding cable.

1. Purchase grounding cable. It will look like a long black cord with one end that plugs into the ground portion of an outlet, and the other

end with an alligator clip.

2. Locate the metal on the bed that you are going to ground. In most cases this is the bed frame itself.

3. Clamp the alligator clip to the metal bed frame.

4. Plug in the grounding cable into the ground portion of the outlet nearest the bed.

5. Hide cable so that it is out of sight and not easily tripped on.

After following those five steps, your bed frame is now grounded. If your box spring is the only metal on your bed, then you will have to make a small cut on the bottom side of it. Once you made the cut, locate one of the metal springs and clamp the alligator clip to it. Then continue on with step 4. Having a bed that is grounded means that rather than the excess electricity being attracted to the metal and eventually making its way into your body, it will follow the path of least resistance, the ground portion of your outlet. In order to confirm that the grounding cable is working, remeasure the body voltage in bed. Your body voltage should have gone down significantly. If it did not, then your problem may be faulty wiring and therefore, following the remediation steps for that is recommended.

Interior remediation "ungrounded 2 prong electronics"-

Most of the devices and appliances within the home that put off high electric fields are ungrounded. You can check to see if a device is grounded by looking at the cable where it plugs into the wall. If there are only 2 prongs on the cable, it is ungrounded. If there are 3 prongs, it is grounded. Anything that is ungrounded will directly impact your body voltage when you are near it, and in some cases if the appliance is large enough it could affect you from the other side of your home. The safest bet for the ungrounded devices in your home is to replace them with a grounded version. This can be as simple as going online, searching "grounded lamp" and replacing it. If you have a MacBook computer, the older models came with a grounded charging cable, the new ones do not. On the Apple website, the grounding adapter is available, but it is pricey. If you are unable to purchase or find the grounded version of the device or appliance that you are currently using, another remediation alternative is to have it "re-corded". There are multiple companies online that allow you to either visit their store in person, or send your device or appliance through the mail. Once they receive it, they take off the ungrounded cord and replace it with a grounded version. However, you must specify that you want a grounded cable. I have had some clients who have sent their lamps in only to have them returned with an ungrounded cable attached.

Interior remediation "power strips"-

In some of the homes that I have conducted inspections for, I have seen multiple power strips linked together forming what is called a "daisy chain". This should never be used in the absence of an extension cord due to the fact that it can cause injury. When used properly, the electric field coming from a single power strip can be high. However, that is not the case with all power strips. What I have found is that some power strips put off high electric fields, while others are actually designed to be "surge protectors" and therefore protect against high electric fields. If your home has a power strip that is putting off high electric fields, the cheapest remediation step is to discontinue its use. If that is not an option and you need a power strip for all of the devices that you require to be in use, then the other remediation step is to replace it with a "surge protector" version. Although there are a lot of these on the market, only about half of them actually do what they say they do. So, if you are replacing yours, make sure that you check the return policy of the one you are looking to purchase. Then, you can try it out with your electric field meter and determine if it is a suitable replacement.

Interior remediation "house shoes"-

If you are looking to eliminate your electrical field even further and lower your body voltage within your home, then I urge you to purchase a pair of shoes that you only wear inside of your house. I call these "house shoes". When measuring body voltage, it is a good idea to take measurements with your shoes on and your shoes off inside of the property. In most cases, you will notice that with your shoes off and standing still, your body voltage will be significantly higher. That is because the electricity flowing through your walls and floor are attracted to your body. Without shoes on, it is easier for the electricity to make its way into your body via your feet. By wearing shoes inside you will notice that your body voltage is lower. If you do not allow shoes inside of your house, then purchasing a separate pair of shoes that is only worn inside will help lower your body voltage. If you do not care about tracking dirt inside of your home, then just continue to wear shoes indoors when possible.

Interior remediation "computer"-

Something that is often missed during most home inspections is the electric field coming from an ungrounded computer. While sitting in front of a laptop computer, you may notice that your body voltage goes up significantly when placing your hand on the keyboard. This can be remediated if the charger for your laptop is grounded. If it is grounded, plug it into the wall outlet so that the laptop is charging. By doing so, your body voltage and electric field will be less than if it were not plugged in. If your laptop charger is not grounded, there is a simple solution available on LessEMF.com called a "computer grounding cable". This cable plugs into a USB port of your laptop and then plugs into a standard wall outlet, grounding it. If your computer does not have a USB port, then the next remediation solution is to look online for the grounded version of your computer charger.

Interior remediation "holiday lights"-

During the holidays, putting up strings of lights is somewhat of a standard tradition in most households. Unfortunately, these seemingly harmless holiday lights have been proven to raise body voltage significantly. For example, in my home we put up holiday lights on the exterior and interior of the property. Although they looked nice, my fiancé wanted to run an experiment to see if having them on would affect our body voltage while sitting on the couch less than 6 feet away. With the lights on, our body voltage was approximately 250mV while sitting on the couch. Standing next to the lights (wrapped around a Christmas tree), our body voltage was 3000mV. With the lights unplugged, our body voltage sitting on the couch was 75mV and standing next to the tree was 250mV. After discovering that the lights were unsafe to have on while sitting on the couch or standing near the tree, we decided to unplug the lights. Unfortunately, there are no "low EMF" holiday lights available on the market that I know of. So, if you have holiday lights up, make sure that you test the electric field and body voltage with them plugged in. If the levels are above safe range, the only remediation step you can take is to leave the lights unplugged. If that is not an option, then move the lights to an area of your home where you are not affected.

Interior remediation "electric stove"-

When cooking on an electric stove top, your body voltage will go up and the electric field will be extremely high. For remediation there are two options. The first and most effective is to replace your electric stove top for a gas stove. If that is not possible then the next remediation option is to use the back row of burners rather than the front row, and stand away from the electric stove top while it is in use. Remember, electric fields extend outward approximately 6-8 feet from the source. Therefore, by standing as far away as possible and using the back burners, you should be outside of the electric field. Just to make sure though, take measurements while the stove is on, and determine at which distance you are safe to stand while it is in use.

After completing the electric field remediation portion of your home inspection, go back around the exterior and interior of the property and re check your work. You should also compare the baseline inspection measurements to the remediation measurements. Then, make sure that there are no other sources of electric fields on the property and that the meter reading remains as close to zero as possible. Once you have confirmed that the electric fields are as close to zero as possible, and the results of the remediation are documented in the remediation section of the inspection form, you are now ready to continue on with the final step of the inspection.

Steps 10 & 11-

Dirty Electricity Inspection and Remediation

Checking a home for dirty electricity is extremely simple, but finding its source can be quite difficult. The meter itself is plugged into a wall outlet and the amount of dirty electricity is measured one outlet at a time. This step is usually left for last simply because of its difficulty. If you are looking for the fastest, cheapest, most effective way of eliminating dirty electricity, then cutting the power at the breaker box is the best option. No electricity means that you don't have to worry about it being dirty or not. However, most of my clients would rather spend the money fixing the problem than putting a temporary band aid on it. For example, I spent hours inside one of my client's homes turning off devices, unplugging motorized appliances and was only able to eliminate approximately 20% of the dirty electricity flowing through the wiring inside of his home. Since that wasn't enough to make a difference, I then began adding special filters that are designed to clean up the dirty electricity at the outlet itself. Yet, that only eliminated an additional 30% of the problem, bringing the total reduction of dirty electricity to 50%. I tried everything that I could think of inside of the home that didn't involve spending large amounts of money to rewire it properly. Eventually, he agreed to allow me to shut the power off at the breaker box in order to eliminate the dirty electricity inside of his bedroom. This was merely a temporary solution in order to prove to him that the problem could be fixed. After a few nights of sleeping without the power to his bedroom, all of his previous health complaints were nonexistent, proving that the problem was dirty electricity. The next week he invested in a device that cleans up dirty electricity out at the breaker box and was able to switch back on the power to his room without his health complaints returning.

As you can see from the example above, the process of eliminating dirty electricity can be quite difficult, but if done correctly can make a large difference in the overall effectiveness of the individuals results. Throughout this chapter you will learn what dirty electricity is, how to measure it, and how to ultimately eliminate it.

Dirty electricity is created by excess oscillation and spikes of frequencies exceeding 60hz while traveling from one point to another. It is a poorly understood part of the EMF spectrum by some professionals due to its seemingly complex way of occurring. Fortunately for you, it is not as complex as it seems and can be easily understood by looking at the example on the following page.

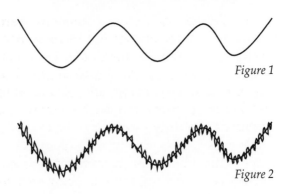

Figure 1

Figure 2

In figure 1 what you are looking at is a standard sine wave. This is what your electricity flowing through your walls and into your devices should look like, smooth and even peaks and valleys oscillating at a consistent flow. When the electricity is "dirty", it will look more like figure 2. Notice how in figure 2 the sine wave looks "spikey" or "fuzzy"? This is because the levels of electricity are not consistent and are fluctuating at extremely fast rates while still trying to follow a standard sine wave oscillation. In most homes today, figure 2 is what I see. This results in multiple problems ranging from blown devices and appliances to higher electricity bills. What concerns me most is not the damage done to appliances or the impact made on electricity bills, but the health effects that occur in the presence of dirty electricity. In the book *Dirty Electricity* author Sam Milham studied the adverse health effects on people as an epidemiologist. In one example he discusses how dirty electricity and attention disorders are associated. He further explains how a teacher inside of her classroom was able to control the behavior of the students by installing "dirty electricity filters". When the filters were installed, the children within her classroom were calm, paid attention, and were overall less disruptive. Then, the teacher took out the filters and within 30 minutes the behavior of the children made a complete opposite change. Needless to say, the results were astonishing and have been replicated numerous times in various peer reviewed studies.

Dirty electricity seems to be a major problem in most of the homes that I have inspected. It is created through the inversion process used with solar panels, CFL and other fluorescent light bulbs, dimmer switches, and any other sources that alternate the flow of electricity. Due to its relatively unique status, unfortunately there are no safety standards in place by any governing body to safeguard the consumer. However, there are numerous companies that have developed ways of measuring dirty electricity and two in particular that have set their own recommended safety standards. Below I have included the safety standard of one of those companies as well as my personal recommendation based off of my own experience:

1. < 25 mV = GreenWave Company
2. < 20 mV = My recommendation

The most common sources that cause dirty electricity can best be understood by breaking them down into two separate categories: Exterior and Interior.

*Most common **exterior** sources*

1. Solar panel inverters
2. Neighbors home

3. Electrical power substation

*Most common **interior** sources*

1. Compact Fluorescent Lights (CFL)
2. Fluorescent Lights
3. Chargers
4. Dimmer Switches

Throughout this section you will learn how to inspect a home for dirty electricity as well as how to remediate if necessary. In my experience, every home in the United States that I have inspected has had dirty electricity. Some homes are worse than others, and require much more attention, while the majority of homes are remediated in a matter of minutes. No matter how good or bad your dirty electricity levels are, I can assure you that you will find them, and you will remediate them. Below I have broken down what you will be doing during the dirty electricity inspection portion of the EMF home inspection. The following 3 steps will be discussed in detail throughout the chapter:

Step 1- Establish Baseline
Step 2- Exterior of the property
Step 3- Interior of the property

Step 1- Establish Baseline

If you are following this guide the way it has been laid out, then you have now reached the final portion of the EMF home inspection. Which means that you should have already completed the baseline measurements of the dirty electricity levels on the exterior and interior of the property. By now, the remediation steps you have taken for radio frequencies, magnetic fields and electric fields, may have changed your initial baseline measurement of dirty electricity. This is due to the fact that by remediating one area of the EMF spectrum, other areas are directly impacted. Therefore, it is a good idea to make sure that your baseline measurements have been documented prior to starting any inspection or remediation. If you haven't completed your baseline measurement of dirty electricity the measurements at this point may be skewed, but should be completed nonetheless. If you have completed the baseline measurements, please continue on to step number 2.

Step 2- Exterior of property

Inspecting the exterior of the property for dirty electricity is accomplished through a meter as well as through observation. Begin by starting at the front of the property and looking around at the surrounding area. What do you see? How close are the neighbors? Do the neighbors have solar panels? Is there a power substation nearby? Truly observe the exterior of the property. What you are looking for is any source that may impact the dirty electricity of the property. If the home is near neighbors with solar panels, or near a power substation, chances are that the dirty electricity levels on the interior of the property are going to be high. For example, one of my clients contacted me because her health took a turn for the worst. She went from doctor to doctor trying to figure out what was wrong with her but each one came up with the same diagnosis: stress. Being that she was in her 60's and had no reason to stress, she didn't accept her diagnosis and decided to try and figure it out on her own. That is when she found out about dirty electricity and thought possibly it could be the culprit. Upon arriving at her property, I immediately noticed that the neighbor on the right of her had solar panels. Which meant that more than likely her dirty electricity levels were going to be high on the inside of her house. In the end I was correct and her levels of dirty electricity were through the roof on the interior of her property. After remediation, her symptoms disappeared and she no longer is confused for being "stressed" by her doctors.

Once you have looked around the exterior of the front of the property for any sources that may generate dirty electricity, next you will try and locate an outlet. Typically, there are two total outlets on the exterior of the average home. One in the front of the property, and the other in the backyard. After locating the outlet in the front of the property, plug in the dirty electricity meter and document your results in the inspection column of the inspection form. If the results are higher than 25mV, you have a dirty electricity problem.

Next, move to the sides of the home and observe the surroundings just as you did in the front of the property. If you haven't looked before, then take a good look at your neighbor's home. Do they have solar panels? You will notice multiple smart meters on the side of the house as well as numerous extra metal boxes if they have solar. If *your* home has solar panels, then you will notice the solar panel equipment on the side of the house. Once you have observed the sides of the home, make sure to write down any observations that may directly impact the dirty electricity levels. For example:

- *Neighbors on left side of home have solar panels.*
- *Substation located on right side of home.*

If there are any outlets on the side of the home, make sure to plug in the dirty electricity meter and document the measurements as well. Then, move on to the backyard. Look around once again and see if there are any neighbors with solar panels or if you are near a power substation. In some rare cases, you may be unfortunate enough to live near a cell phone tower. If that is the case, there have been times where the amount of dirty electricity is directly impacted due to the presence of that cell tower (as well as other areas of the EMF spectrum). After looking around and observing your surroundings, next you will locate any outlets in the backyard. Like I said before, the average home has at least one outlet in the backyard, but some have more. Plug the dirty electricity meter into any and all of the outlets that are in the backyard, and document the measurements.

That's it for the exterior of the property. There isn't a whole lot to it. Once you have completed all of the exterior inspection and documentation, next you will head to the interior of the property.

Step 3- Interior of property

Starting in room number 1, locate all of the outlets within the room and begin plugging in the meter to measure the dirty electricity levels one at a time in a clockwise pattern. Since each home is different, the levels of dirty electricity will vary. However, on average the dirty electricity levels within most of the homes I have inspected, pre remediation, is around 350mV. In homes with serious dirty electricity problems, the levels have maxed out my meter (>2,000mV). Remember though, if your readings are above 25mV, you have a dirty electricity problem and remediation is necessary.

With the dirty electricity meter plugged into the first outlet in room number 1, I look around for any dimmer switches that may be in the room. In most homes I typically will see a few and therefore test them while my meter is plugged in. Having a dimmer switch is like putting a cap on the amount of electricity that is being supplied to the light. Rather than a switch where 100% of the power is supplied when on and 0% is supplied when off, a dimmer switch lets you determine how much "percent" you want to supply. While this may seem nice, it actually creates a massive amount of dirty electricity.

Next, I turn on the lights within the room in order to determine the type of lightbulb that is being used. If you are unable to determine the type of lightbulb it is by its brightness and color, then turn the light off, unscrew the lightbulb and read the label. In some cases, the label will only include a model number. If that is the case then type the model number into your ethernet enabled computer in order to determine the type of lightbulb you are using. In all of the homes that I have completed home inspections for, the main lightbulb that is used is a CFL or Compact Fluorescent Lightbulb. These are popular because of their energy saving capability. However, the way they save energy is by turning on and off thousands of times per second, which saves energy but increases the amount of dirty electricity within the home significantly. Seeing this in action is actually quite remarkable. With your meter plugged into an outlet, turn the light on within the room. If it is a CFL, you will see the dirty electricity rise on the meter.

After completing room number 1 and documenting your findings under the inspection column, grab your dirty electricity meter and head to room number 2. In most homes this room is the kitchen, which just so happens to be the number one room for dirty electricity. The main problems you will run into in this room are from CFL or Fluorescent Lightbulbs, and from appliances or devices that are ungrounded and plugged in. If the kitchen you are inspecting has these style lights, you will notice the dirty electricity levels being extremely high when the meter is plugged in and the lights are on. However, in some of the kitchens I have inspected, the levels of dirty electricity are so high that there is no noticeable difference with the lights on or off. And although the average dirty electricity levels are around 350mV in most homes, the kitchen levels tend to average 200mV higher than the rest of the home (550mV). This can easily be remediated.

After checking the lights, plug the dirty electricity meter into one of the outlets within the kitchen and begin using the standard appliances that you would use on a daily basis. If you are a coffee drinker, plug the coffee maker into the outlet where the meter is located and turn it on. Note if the levels of dirty electricity go up, and then move on to the next appliance. If you use a blender every morning for smoothies, plug that in next and note the dirty electricity levels. Continue this pattern until you have used all of the appliances or devices that you would use inside of your kitchen, documenting your results on your inspection form. The pattern that you should notice is that anything that is ungrounded or runs on A/C (alternating current), the dirty electricity levels will go up.

Once the kitchen is complete, continue on to the next rooms with your dirty electricity meter. Locate every outlet within the room and measure them one at a time. Make sure to take measurements with the lights on and off and document the results. At this point I usually start counting how many CFL lights there are in each room so that when it comes to the remediation step, I know how many that will need to be replaced. In the bathrooms you will notice the main problems coming from the lighting, the ventilation fan, and the blow dryer. Make sure that you are testing each of these items by turning them on and off while the dirty electricity meter is plugged in.

On the way to the next room, make sure to check any of the appliances or devices that are in the hallways by plugging them in and turning them on and off while the dirty electricity meter is also plugged in. If there is a vacuum, turn it on and note the dirty electricity levels while it is in use. If there are lamps in the hallway, plug the dirty electricity meter in and then turn the lamp on. Test everything and anything that is used on a regular basis. Although this may sound excessive, I can assure you that it is necessary. What you are looking for is anything that may cause the dirty electricity levels to rise. In most homes, the devices that are tucked away in drawers or closets have been some of the worst culprits of dirty electricity. Therefore, by testing everything, you are able to determine what may need to be replaced for a safer version during the remediation step.

When you arrive at a bedroom, the main problems that you will run into are from the lighting and from devices that are ungrounded. If there are lamps on the nightstands, I like to show the client just how much dirty electricity they produce with a little experiment. For this, unplug the lamps located on the nightstand and then plug your dirty electricity meter into the top outlet. Then, plug the lamp back in to the bottom outlet but keep it off. In most cases the levels will rise just by plugging in the lamp. Then, turn the lamp on. With the lamp on the levels will spike even higher. This is because the lamp is most likely ungrounded and anything that is ungrounded will create a high amount of dirty electricity.

If the home being inspected has solar panels, the amount of dirty electricity will most likely be too high for your meter to read. This is due to the inverter. What an inverter does is convert the energy from the sun from A/C (alternating current) to D/C (direct current). During this process the amount of electricity is essentially funneled from the massive amount provided by the sun's energy to an amount usable by your devices. However, the amount that is funneled is not always the amount that is needed to power your devices. Instead you are receiving thousands of more times the amount needed, which can result in your devices overheating, and ultimately your health being affected. In homes with solar panels the average dirty electricity levels are above 2,000mV (under 25mV is safe).

Once you have fully inspected the home for dirty electricity by checking each and every outlet, the next step is to make sure that all of your documentation is in order. If you have properly noted all of the various dirty electricity levels, and documented the devices or appliances that have caused levels to exceed safe limits, the next step is remediation.

Remediation

When remediating a home of dirty electricity, I always start with offering the option that is free. I do this for one reason, fixing dirty electricity can be very expensive and depending on the individual, they may not have a lot to spend. For example, one of my clients was having a difficult time getting pregnant and had read the book *Dirty Electricity* by Sam Milham. In his book the author discusses a bank where all of the women were struggling to get pregnant. After determining that the business had a dirty electricity problem, special filters were installed to filter out the dirty electricity. Months later, all of the women went out on maternity leave at the same time. Wanting to know if her problem with getting pregnant could be related to dirty electricity she contacted me and had me conduct an inspection. We talked a lot about the effects dirty electricity has on our health and after revealing that she had a significant problem with dirty electricity the topic of solutions came up during remediation. Unfortunately, the $500.00 price tag of the filters discussed in the book was a little too steep for her. So, I offered her a free alternative. A few months later she was pregnant and concluded the lack of dirty electricity was the reason. After that she invested the $500.00 on the filters and has never been happier. Below you will learn how to remediate the most common sources of dirty electricity on the exterior and interior of your home. As a reminder, the most common sources are listed here:

*Most common **exterior** sources*

1. Solar panel inverters
2. Neighbors home
3. Electrical power substation

*Most common **interior** sources*

1. Compact Fluorescent Lights (CFL)
2. Fluorescent Lights
3. Chargers
4. Dimmer Switches

Exterior remediation "Solar panel inverters"-

Being EHS (Electromagnetic Hypersensitivity) I have somewhat of an advantage when it comes to inspecting and remediating homes. My body can literally sense when an environment is unsuitable to be in. Usually, if I am in an environment with dirty electricity for longer than a few hours, I start feeling as if I have drunk 10 energy drinks, my head pounds, I get extremely dehydrated, and have trouble concentrating on a single task. For example, I recently moved into my fiancé's parents' home as a temporary solution until the building of our EMF free community is complete. Up until the time of moving in, I had spent numerous occasions at their house and had remediated it of EMFs, making it extremely safe to spend time in. However, the one issue that still remained was that they had solar panels. Attempts to remediate this problem were made prior to moving in by installing GreenWave filters in every outlet of their home. Unfortunately, the filters caused the breaker to short circuit due to the massive amount of electricity coming in from the solar panels. Which meant that whenever they plugged in the filters, the power would turn off in their entire house. Although the instructions said to allow this to occur until the electricity is filtered completely, they didn't want to have to keep going out to the breaker box every time it tripped. So, they invested in a device that attaches out at the breaker box called a "power perfect box". This device filters out the dirty electricity right at the breaker box prior to it coming into the house. After getting it installed, I expected the dirty electricity levels to drop drastically but instead they went from above 2,000mV to 1,800mV. But it was too late because I had already moved in to their house expecting the dirty electricity to not be a problem anymore. After one night of "sleeping" at their house I woke up feeling extremely sick. That was the first time that I had ever spent that much time around solar panels and that high of levels of dirty electricity. After that, my fiancé called the solar panel company (with the permission of her parents) and learned how to turn the solar panels off. With the solar panels off, the power perfect box really began to shine. The results of the measured difference are listed below:

Solar panels ON: >2,000mV

Solar panels OFF: 900mV
Power Perfect Box ON: 16mV

As you can see, the results of the remediation were remarkable. From that point on I haven't had a single night of bad sleep, not to mention that her parents are sleeping better than they have in a very long time.

If your home has solar panels, as you have learned from the example above, there are a few remediation steps that you can take in order to make your home safe from dirty electricity. Ultimately however, the most effective method is to turn them off completely. Below I have listed the three different options you can take for remediating solar panels.

1. GreenWave dirty electricity filters- These filters work by plugging directly into the outlet that has dirty electricity. It's that simple, just plug it in and watch on your dirty electricity meter as the numbers drop immediately. However, multiple of these filters are required in order to make any difference and with one costing $30.00 on Amazon it can be a little pricey. On average, I install 10 of these filters per home that I inspect. If the home doesn't have solar panels, that is typically all that is needed to reduce the dirty electricity levels. On homes that have solar, more are definitely needed but may not be as effective as a power perfect box. Also, due to the capacitors working overtime inside of the filter, a small magnetic field is produced. If you are going to install these, make sure to go back and measure the

magnetic field with your magnetic field meter after installing them. On average this field extends out about 12" from the outlet in the homes that I have tested. If you have installed filters inside of your home and the circuits are tripping causing power loss, follow the instructions that come with the filter and wait until the inverter adjusts, or choose an alternative remediation technique.

2. Power Perfect Box- These devices are very amazing. If you are going to install one of these in an attempt to lower your dirty electricity, just a warning, it is very expensive. If your home has solar then you must purchase the one that is designed for solar, which cost approximately $1,600.00. On top of that you need to hire an electrician to install it which costs on average $100.00 per hour. Then you have to purchase a breaker to attach to the power perfect box and the breaker panel which can cost up to $20.00. All in all, installation of this box can cost up to $2,000.00. With that being said, it can make a difference on the amount of dirty electricity created by the solar panels within your home. However, it will not lower it to safe levels. If you are in a home that does not have solar panels, having one of these installed is highly recommended. Not just because it filters out dirty electricity extremely well without solar panels, but because it pretty much pays for itself. By filtering out dirty electricity, your devices run better and last longer, and you actually save money on your utility bill. I would say that average savings is around 10% of your total

bill a month. Which after a few years, pays for itself. Plus, the owners of the company are so confident that it is going to work for you, that you can install it on your house, see the difference for yourself, and if you aren't pleased with the results, you can return it for a full refund. However, it is always a good idea to contact them first before installing it and ask for a guarantee.

3. Turn off solar- If you have tried the above two remediation steps and still haven't seen a major reduction in the levels of dirty electricity then the only option left is to turn off your solar panels. This step can be a little tricky. The solar companies tend to not want you to discontinue service with them and will often not allow you to turn them off. That was until I developed a script that has worked flawlessly. Before I get into the script, if you are truly interested in lowering the levels of dirty electricity within your home, then getting rid of solar is crucial. However, consider this step a "trial" and only turn your solar panels off for a month. If at the end of the month you are not feeling a difference, call your solar company back and have them walk you through the steps necessary to turn your solar panels back on. When you contact your solar company to have them turned off, do not say "I want to turn off my solar panels." Instead the script that you will use is "I am having some work done on the exterior of my house and need to know how to turn off the inverter temporarily." They will then walk you through how to turn off your solar panels.

Once the system is off, head back inside with your dirty electricity filter and take measurements of the levels with your meter. After that, if you have a power perfect box installed, turn it off and take measurements, then turn it on and take measurements. This will be the only way for you to see if the remediation steps taken have worked. Also, if you have GreenWave filters installed, make sure to unplug them and take measurements of the dirty electricity with your meter again. By turning off your solar panels, your baseline measurements will change.

Exterior remediation "neighbors' home"-

If you are close with your neighbors, this remediation step can be quite fun. In most of the homes that I have inspected, when I plug the dirty electricity meter into the wall, I can hear what their neighbors are watching on television or listening to on their stereo/radio. This is because the electricity that you are using in your home is essentially recycled from the neighbors next to you and yours is recycled to the neighbors next to you as well. This is even more apparent in hotels and apartment buildings. For example, one of my clients lived in an apartment building on the top floor. When measuring the dirty electricity levels inside of her bedroom, rather than hearing the standard static of what the electricity sounds like, *Law and Order* the television show started playing through the meter. Immediately my client knew where it was coming from and said "oh that's probably just the neighbor below me." She then opened the window to the balcony and sure enough, you could hear the television going from the apartment below. In hotel rooms it's even worse. If while measuring the dirty electricity levels within your home you hear what your neighbors are watching or listening to, and you are close with your neighbors, I urge you to go over to their house and confirm what your meter is picking up. Once you are done having your fun, remediating this can be extremely easy. Install a power perfect box or install GreenWave filters. Both of these devices will filter out the dirty electricity from the exterior of your home.

Exterior remediation "electrical power substation"-

If you live near an electrical power substation, you may already know the negative effects they have on your health. Remediating against the dirty electricity caused from living near a substation is more difficult than remediating a home with solar panels. Installation of a power perfect box will help filter out a good percentage coming from the substation, but will not lower the dirty electricity to below 25mV. For that to occur, chances are that you will need to install an additional power perfect box as well as install GreenWave filters at every outlet on the interior of the house. If this is not enough to remediate the problem, then the only other option is to move to a home that is not near an electrical power substation.

Interior remediation "CFL or fluorescent lightbulbs"-

If your home has CFL or fluorescent lightbulbs, there is only one remediation step necessary. Get rid of them and replace them with incandescent lightbulbs. Unfortunately, these types of lightbulbs are not available in stores anymore and must be ordered online.

For those of you who are looking to cut down your exposure levels even more, you do have the option of cutting the power to any room where you do not want dirty electricity at all. This option is free and is what I tend to offer most clients as a way to "try it before you buy it." If you cut the power to your bedroom for example, you are no longer going to have dirty electricity (or electric fields or magnetic fields) and therefore are able to determine if you feel better in that type of environment. When you feel the results, investing in various products will be justified. If you are wondering about the effects of CFL or fluorescent lightbulbs, prior to purchasing new bulbs, try only using soy wax candles at night for a month. Once you see the difference, investing in new lightbulbs will also be justified.

Interior remediation "chargers"-

Most chargers today are ungrounded and therefore put off massive amounts of dirty electricity. If you are charging your cell phone with an ungrounded 2-prong charger in one room, the dirty electricity will be affected all over the house. I have seen situations where a simple iPhone charger being unplugged will drop the dirty electricity levels by 80%. So, for this remediation step, go around the house and unplug any charger that you see. Then, go back around and remeasure the levels of dirty electricity. They should have dropped. If they haven't, next you will go around and unplug anything else that is plugged into your walls. Typically, I like to do this one device at a time but for this it requires 2 people. If you have a partner willing to assist you with this step, then follow the steps below:

1. Person number 1 will plug the dirty electricity meter into an outlet that has a very high reading and stand with it in their hand.
2. Person number 2 will walk around the room and unplug any device, appliance or charger one at a time.
3. After each device, appliance or charger is unplugged person number 1 will read the dirty electricity levels out loud.
4. If the numbers didn't go down, person number 2 will walk into other rooms and repeat step 2.
5. Once something is unplugged where the readings go down significantly, person number 1 and 2 will meet up and discuss their findings.

In most homes the devices that put off the most dirty electricity are cell phone and computer chargers. If that is the case with your home, replacing them with grounded versions or leaving them unplugged are your only options for remediation.

Interior remediation "dimmer switches"-

If you have dimmer switches installed and are a source for dirty electricity in your home, then hiring an electrician to replace them is recommended for remediation. Typically, it will cost less than $100.00 to replace all of the dimmer switches in your home and will take less than an hour.

Interior remediation "still high"-

If you have replaced lightbulbs, unplugged chargers and ungrounded devices, removed dimmer switches, and your levels of dirty electricity are still high then you have two options for remediation. First, install GreenWave filters in the majority of the outlets, or second, hire an electrician to install a power perfect box on the exterior of the home.

After you have completed the dirty electricity remediation, go back around the home and take measurements. Then, document what the remediation levels are now at. This will ensure that if anything changes, you have documentation to support your theory. If for example your neighbors get solar panels installed, you will be able to determine if further remediation is necessary to protect against their recycled dirty electricity. It is also a good idea to measure levels during random times of the day and night. This will also guarantee that your remediation steps were effective.

Steps 12 & 13-

Documentation

Congratulations, you have made it to the final steps of conducting your own EMF home inspection. The following steps are some of the most important in regards to your inspection and should never be skipped or passed over. Without documenting your baseline findings, determining if your remediation steps were effective may prove difficult. Although you may want to stop and enjoy your newly remediated home, providing documentation for future comparisons takes little time and will benefit you in the long run. For example, one of my very first clients contacted me with concerns of high radio frequency levels within his home. He had previously purchased his own meter and was taking his own measurements on a daily basis without knowing exactly what he was looking for. I vividly remember asking him "What have you done to remediate the problem?" He responded with "nothing at all, but I know that it is high here." After sending him the pre inspection checklist and researching his home on antennasearch.com, I set up a time for me to come and conduct a home inspection. Within the first 30 minutes of the inspection I located the source of his radio frequency problem and remediated it. My meter read zero, his meter read zero, and we were both happy. A year or so later, he contacted me again claiming that his radio frequency problem had returned but this time was different. He said "whenever I point my meter at my bedroom window it reads off the charts. I think my neighbors got new WiFi. Can you come out and do another inspection for me please?" Being that I am obsessed with documentation, I pulled out his previous readings and began the process all over again. Immediately I found that there had been an increase in cell tower installations around his home, one of which was less than 100 meters away. Without having that previous documentation, I wouldn't have known that a new cell tower had been installed near his home. Of course, after informing him of my findings I went out to his home and did a re inspection, confirming my findings. Everything in his home remained the same, minus the one window on the south side of his bedroom, which just so happened to face the newly installed cell tower. Hopefully by now you have realized the importance of documenting your findings as diligently as possible but just in case you haven't, I have included a few steps below to help you in your journey to becoming a documentation pro.

Step 1- Print out a few copies of the pre inspection checklist and keep them with you just in case the client didn't know how to fill it out, or in case it was filled out incorrectly. Do not rely solely on their documentation. By providing your own copy and filling it out with them (if necessary) you may catch things that they didn't.

Step 2- Print out a copy of the antennasearch.com results as well as the expanded results section showing the map of where the towers and antennas are located in relation to the home. Then, at the top of the printed results, write the date and time that they were printed in legible writing. This provides you with an exact reference point in case new towers are installed. Also, if you download the results found on antennasearch.com, you will notice that the date of each towers installation is provided in an excel spreadsheet.

Step 3- Print out additional copies of the actual inspection form in case you make a mistake and need to start over. Trust me, in the beginning you will make mistakes, and that's okay, just make sure you have additional copies in order to start over and document accurately.

Step 4- Keep scratch paper with you in case you need to make notes that do not need to be given to the client at the end of the inspection.

Step 5- Once the inspection is completed, go over the results of steps 1-3 with the client, making sure to explain them thoroughly. Then offer a typed-up version to the client and inform them that you will be sending it within 24 hours. Some clients however, do not want a typed-up version and prefer the paper version (that is where step 4 comes into play). If they want the paper version of the inspection then see step 6.

Step 6- Create an additional copy of the inspection results on an additional inspection form. It is very important that you do not give them your only copy of the results of the inspection and rely on them to keep it filed away. That way in the future when they contact you again for an additional inspection, you have the results of the first one on hand.

Step 7- This step is for those of you who are overly organized like me, so feel free to skip it if you would like. Once I am back to my office, I create a folder with the clients pre inspection form, antennasearch.com results, and inspection/remediation results. I then write their name on the folder and file it away neatly in my filing cabinet. That way when they contact me in the future for an additional home inspection, I have a copy of their previous inspection results on hand for reference purposes. Since I rarely use a computer, I prefer hard copies of the inspections rather than digital copies. However, you may choose to store your documentation whichever way you please.

After completing the home inspection and remediation (if necessary) I like to keep in touch with the client as well as set up an additional inspection for a future date. This ensures that they are following through with the recommended changes and are living in the best possible environment. Since you are conducting the inspection on your own home, I would recommend setting up monthly inspections of your property. They don't need to be as thorough as the original inspection, but more of a "once over" to make sure things are still the way you left them. Sometimes I have had clients complain of headaches coming back months down the road only for me to come out to their home again and discover that their WiFi was turned back on.

Another client of mine emailed me complaining that they weren't sleeping again and their vibrations were back. Rather than me driving back over to do another home inspection I asked "is your grounding cable still plugged in?" They replied immediately saying "It wasn't plugged in! I think my husband accidentally unplugged it!" After that they were back to getting deep sleep.

Conducting seasonal inspections is also one of the recommendations I make with my clients. During warmer weather more people are using air conditioning, which leads to increased electricity being used and ultimately higher electric fields and body voltage. Personally, my body voltage in bed during the winter is around 70mV and during the summer it is around 145mV. That's even with 90% of my power turned off at the breaker box. It will shock you how different things can change from season to season, and that's why documentation is important. Having a log of past inspections gives you a reference point if something changes. One of my clients for example, had been completing their own monthly inspections after I taught them everything in this guide. They were healthy, happy, and sleeping better than they ever had all because of reducing their home EMF exposure. That was all until one day a 5G cell tower was installed outside of her window on a light post less than 30 feet away from where she slept. Since she had just completed her monthly inspection a few days before it was installed, she had no clue she was being exposed to high amounts of radio frequency radiation. About a week later she contacted me saying:

"I had to do an additional inspection on my house rather than the ones I do monthly because I was getting really dizzy and having bad headaches and brain fog whenever I was home. Do you want to know what I did? I found out that they put a 5G tower outside my bedroom window on the light post and it was blasting me with radio frequencies so high that my meter couldn't pick it up!"

I immediately had her leave her house and set up a time for me to come and see if remediation was possible. So, as you can see, a one-time home inspection is good, but checking at a minimum of once monthly is recommended. Things change, new technology gets installed, and unless you are monitoring your home often you could end up paying the price years later with your health.

Conclusion

~

If you are reading this guide and have completed your own home inspection and have seen positive results then I urge you to pay it forward. Either lend someone you know who could benefit from this a copy of the guide, or conduct a home inspection for them. In the early stages of developing this guide I had clients ask me for copies so that they could leave them on their neighbors' porch, hoping my words would influence them to change their lifestyle and inadvertently change the environment around their home. On one occasion, I had a client who was in the process of selling his house and during an open house his neighbors stopped by to "take a look at his set up." When they entered, one of them said "it feels like I'm at the beach", referring to how calm she felt inside the home. After explaining that his home was EMF proof, my client handed her a copy of this guide and instructed her on how to make her home feel the same way. Not to mention that the remediation cost was recouped after he sold his house due to the fact that it was seen as an improvement to the home and one of the main selling points.

By now you should have a firm understanding of the steps necessary to conducting your very own EMF home inspection. However, before I end this guide, I would like to make one additional recommendation. Get to know yourself better by keeping a journal. Some of my clients laugh when I make this recommendation but, in the end, they always thank me. For example, one of my clients set up a home inspection for her son. She had read my first book *EHS Warrior: Beating Mold Illness, Lyme Disease, and Electromagnetic Hypersensitivity*, and noticed many similarities in my story to her son. For years she spent hundreds of thousands of dollars trying to cure her son of Lyme Disease with little to no success. After learning that EMFs could potentially be the problem, she contacted me and said "he's on his phone all day and all night, he uses Bluetooth headphones, and surfs the internet on his laptop at the same time. His numbers are not as bad as yours were, but his symptoms are the exact same. Could he benefit from an EMF home inspection?"

When I arrived at her home to conduct the EMF home inspection, her son was glued to his cell phone and immediately I noticed the similarities in symptoms that she had talked about. He looked like a zoned-out zombie, made little to no eye contact, and barely had enough energy to get a word out. Most parents would agree that that behavior is typical for their children now a days, but my client knew a different version of her son. Prior to getting sick he was extremely active and rarely used technology. After discussing his story and comparing it to my own, I asked him if he kept a journal. He laughed. Apparently, keeping a journal isn't considered "cool" anymore. That is when things got interesting. He looked right in my eyes and said "I am willing to try anything if it means getting my life back again." So, I pulled out a blank journal (something I keep with me during home inspections for situations just like this), and asked for him to "get to know himself a little better." After conducting the home inspection and remediating his environment, making it suitable for someone in his condition to heal, I explained what I wanted him to write about. I said:

"When I was sick, I thought the exact same way as you. I was willing to try anything and everything if it meant getting myself back to a healthy point. I heard about the dangers of EMFs and then analyzed my lifestyle and determined that a digital detox could benefit me in more than one way. Instead of using my phone or computer, I opted for a pen and journal. I began writing my story and all the things I tried to get better, eventually turning it into a book. That's how I got here today, your mom read my book and thought we had a similar story. Maybe you can spend some time writing your story and getting to know yourself a little better."

His eyes lit up and he said "if you can do it, I can do it." A few months later I received a letter in the mail from him. Rather than spend his time writing his story, he decided to write letters to everyone in his life that had helped him, informing everyone of his new EMF free lifestyle. He further explained that a majority of his symptoms had completely disappeared and that he was more aware of how he felt around certain wireless devices, ending with "Thank you for helping me get to know myself again."

Now I'm not saying that you can cure diseases by living in a reduced EMF home environment, I can't make a claim like that. However, every single person I have conducted an EMF home inspection for has seen some sort of improvement in their lifestyle. By keeping a journal and documenting your life before and after remediation, you may notice something that you weren't aware of before. Unfortunately, you will never know unless you conduct an EMF home inspection yourself. Good luck, and I wish you all the best in health and in happiness.

References

~

Listed below are various websites, books, and movies that can be used to further improve your knowledge on EMFs.

Website- Environmental Health Trust: Ehtrust.org

Website- Less EMF: LessEMF.com

Book- *The Invisible Rainbow* by Arthur Firstenburg

Book- *EMF Freedom* by Elizabeth Plourde, PhD and Marcus Plourde, PhD

Book- Dirty Electricity by Samuel Milham, MD, MPH

Movie- Take back your power (available for free on youtube.com)

Movie- Generation Zapped (available on Amazon)

Photo Credit

~

The photos provided in this guide were taken and edited by Max Tuta Noronha. His work can be seen on his website listed below:

www.maxtutanoronha.com

The textures Max used were provided by Philippe Sainte-Laudy. His work can be seen on his website listed below:

www.naturephotographie.com

Forms and Extras

~

Quick Reference Guide

Pre-Inspection Form

Inspection Form

Excerpt from *EHS Warrior: Beating Mold Illness, Lyme Disease, and Electromagnetic Hypersensitivity*

DIY EMF HOME INSPECTION GUIDE

Quick Reference Guide

Step 1- Purchase necessary EMF detecting meters.

Step 2- Fill out necessary pre inspection checklist, and look up your home or space you are inspecting on the website antennasearch.com.

Step 3- Conduct baseline measurement of exterior and interior of home or space you are inspecting prior to starting the actual inspection.

Step 4- Conduct **exterior** inspection with radio frequency meter and remediate if necessary.

Step 5- Conduct **interior** inspection with radio frequency meter and remediate if necessary.

Step 6- Conduct **exterior** inspection with magnetic field meter and remediate if necessary.

Step 7- Conduct **interior** inspection with magnetic field meter and remediate if necessary.

Step 8- Conduct **exterior** inspection with electric field meter and body voltage meter and remediate if necessary.

Step 9- Conduct **interior** inspection electric field meter and body voltage meter and remediate if necessary.

Step 10- Conduct **exterior** inspection with dirty electricity meter (if home has exterior outlets) and remediate if necessary.

Step 11- Conduct **interior** inspection with dirty electricity meter and remediate if necessary.

Step 12- Make sure documentation is provided with baseline measurements as well as after remediation measurements.

Step 13- Set up a future date to conduct a reinspection of the above steps again. This can be done weekly, monthly or annually depending on your individual needs.

Pre-Inspection Form

In order to gain an accurate representation of your current EMF use, whether intentional or unintentional, please fill out the below questionnaire to the best of your ability.

Exterior of House

1. Are there any above ground power lines near your property?
2. Do you have a smart meter? (I.e. gas, electric, water)
3. Can you see a cell tower from anywhere on your property?
4. Do you have solar panels?
5. Are your neighbors' homes close enough to pick up their Wi-Fi?
6. Do you have a wireless security/doorbell system?
7. Do you have any exterior Bluetooth enabled devices? (i.e. pool lighting, anything that can be controlled by an app on your phone)

Interior of House

1. Do you have Wi-Fi?
2. Do you have a range extender for your Wi-Fi?
3. Do you have a cordless home phone?
4. Do you have a voice automated assistant? (i.e. Alexa, Google assistant)
5. Do you turn your cell phone on "airplane mode" when not in use?
6. Do you have a tablet(s)? (i.e. iPad, kindle)
7. Do you have a "smart tv"?

8. Do you have Bluetooth enabled devices? (i.e. stereo/speakers, headphones, keyboard, mouse, printer, rumba vacuum, tile)
9. Do you have a laptop or home computer?
10. Do you have dimmer switches?
11. Do you leave your electronic appliances plugged in when not in use?
12. Do you use a microwave oven?
13. Do you have an electric stove?
14. Do you have fluorescent/halogen light bulbs?
15. Do you use a hair dryer?
16. Do you use an electric razor or electric toothbrush?
17. Do you have "smart appliances"?
18. Do you sleep near a plugged-in lamp?
19. Do you have a plugged-in alarm clock near where you sleep?
20. Has there ever been mold damage in your home?
21. Do you have a Wi-Fi enabled thermostat? (i.e. Nest)
22. Do you use an electric blanket or electric heating pad?
23. Do you have "smart plugs"?
24. Do you have a Wi-Fi or Bluetooth enabled baby monitor?
25. Do you have a Bluetooth enabled air purifier? (i.e. Molekule)
26. Do you have any video game consoles? (i.e. Xbox, Wii, Nintendo switch, PlayStation)
27. Do you have two or more stories in your home?

Personal

1. Do you carry your cell phone on your body?
2. Do you use speakerphone while talking on your cell phone?
3. Do you wear any "smart" devices? (i.e. Apple Watch, fitness tracker, Fitbit)
4. Do you use Bluetooth enabled headphones?
5. Do you have metal fillings?
6. Do you use metal framed glasses?
7. Do you have any metal in your body? (i.e. metal rod, screws)
8. Do you carry any keyless entry devices on your body? (i.e. car keys)
9. Do you wear a wireless diabetes monitor?
10. Do you have a "smart" or electric car?
11. Do you have Wi-Fi capabilities in your car?
12. Are you using your TV, cell phone, computer or tablet within an hour of falling asleep?

Fill in the blank

1. How many hours a day do you watch television?
2. How many hours a day do you use your cell phone?
3. How many hours a day do you use your computer?
4. How many hours a day do you use your tablet? (i.e. iPad, kindle)
5. How many hours of sleep are you getting per night?
6. Do you have difficulty staying or falling asleep?
7. How long does it take for you to fall asleep?
8. Do you know your body voltage in bed?
9. How many people live in your home?

10. Where is your phone and/or tablet when you are sleeping?
11. How often do you check your cell phone throughout the night?
12. When was the last time you had a home EMF inspection?
13. How many years have you been using a cell phone?
14. How many waking hours per day are you spending technology free?

The intention of the above checklist is to get you thinking of all the EMFs that are currently in your life. Although the list is not fully inclusive, as I do not know your specific situation, it does cover a very large spectrum of average EMF exposure.

Inspection Form

Client Name: _____ Date: _____

Address: _____ Time: _____

Temperature: _____ Weather: _____

Notes:

_____

_____

Exterior of Property

	Baseline	Inspection	Remediation
Radio Frequency North			
Radio Frequency South			
Radio Frequency East			
Radio Frequency West			
Magnetic Field North			
Magnetic Field South			
Magnetic Field East			
Magnetic Field West			

Electric Field North			
Electric Field South			
Electric Field East			
Electric Field West			
Dirty Electricity North			
Dirty Electricity South			
Dirty Electricity East			
Dirty Electricity West			

Interior of Property

	Baseline	Inspection	Remediation
Radio Frequency Room 1			
Radio Frequency Room 2			
Radio Frequency Room 3			
Radio Frequency Room 4			
Radio			

Frequency Room 5			
Radio Frequency Room 6			
Radio Frequency Room 7			
Radio Frequency Room 8			
Radio Frequency Room 9			
Magnetic Field Room 1			
Magnetic Field Room 2			
Magnetic Field Room 3			
Magnetic Field Room 4			
Magnetic Field Room 5			
Magnetic Field Room 6			
Magnetic Field Room 7			
Magnetic Field Room 8			

Magnetic Field Room 9			
Electric Field Room 1			
Electric Field Room 2			
Electric Field Room 3			
Electric Field Room 4			
Electric Field Room 5			
Electric Field Room 6			
Electric Field Room 7			
Electric Field Room 8			
Electric Field Room 9			
Dirty Electricity Room 1			
Dirty Electricity Room 2			
Dirty Electricity			

Room 3			
Dirty Electricity Room 4			
Dirty Electricity Room 5			
Dirty Electricity Room 6			
Dirty Electricity Room 7			
Dirty Electricity Room 8			
Dirty Electricity Room 9			

EHS Warrior

*Beating Mold Illness, Lyme Disease, and
Electromagnetic Hypersensitivity*

Brian R. Humrich, Ph.D.

Chapter 1

My Story

My story does not have a beginning. The unfortunate reason is due to severe memory loss caused by my illness. Instead of a beginning, I will start off by introducing you to what I can remember.

I was driving when all of a sudden, my left shoulder began throbbing with pain. The pain shot from my shoulder, up my neck, and into my jaw. The pain was unusual to say the least. The only thing that seemed to alleviate the pain was applying constant pressure to my shoulder. Due to my history of injuries from weight lifting, I thought I possibly could have torn a muscle or pinched a nerve. The pain continued the rest of my drive home and long into the night. I couldn't sleep, eat or even concentrate due to the constant throbbing.

That night, I stayed up researching the muscles, ligaments, bones and whatever else I could possibly think of that could cause this sort of pain. I was healthy, in great shape, and had no clue what was wrong with me. The possibilities were endless in my opinion. I thought the worst and started creating a list of reasons I could be feeling this excruciating pain. The next morning the pain was gone but in its place was an uneasy feeling. What was that pain I was feeling? Was I imagining it? Was it all just a dream?

The thought of it being a dream began to sink in as I spent the next few days pain free. I felt off but chalked it up to my imagination getting the best of me. A few days later the pain came back but this time it was in my leg. It felt like I had a thousand bees buzzing around the inside of my leg, vibrating from the inside out. This was definitely not a dream. Once again, the fear of the unknown set in and I started to panic. I had no clue what was wrong with me. First, the pain was in one part of my body, now another? How is that even possible? What was the vibrating feeling? Am I dying? The pain was so intense that I couldn't sleep again that night and stayed up researching until the morning. That morning, the pain was gone but once again, the uneasy feeling remained.

That morning I remember feeling as if I had the flu and had the symptoms to match. I had an extremely high fever; I was throwing up nonstop and had severe diarrhea. That's where I thought I had figured out what the mysterious pains were. I thought that I was having body aches as part of the flu. My mind was finally at ease as I remained sick for the next week or so. Well, I was clearly wrong with my self diagnosis and that is where the "fun" began.

When the symptoms of the flu seemed to lessen, a new set of symptoms took its place. I had severe ringing in my ears, my jaw was sore to the touch and my neck was so stiff that I could barely turn from side to side. These new symptoms were like nothing I had ever felt before. My obsessive research to find out what it was, was inconclusive. Trying to explain the pain to other people left me feeling crazy so I kept the symptoms to myself. Looking back, that was a horrible idea. The pain soon made its way to my head, where simple tasks became increasingly difficult. Thinking became painful and talking left me out of breath.

At this point I was under the impression that what I had was rare and couldn't be found through researching online. My head constantly felt heavy with pain, my neck and spine were filled with shooting pains, my hands and arms were shaking constantly, my balance and coordination were completely off, I suddenly became sensitive to lights, and my mind couldn't process what was going on. I felt scared, alone, and a little crazy.

I don't really remember how I got to the point of putting tinfoil on myself to lessen the pain, but somehow, I got there. I had tinfoil in my shoes, under my hat, and all throughout my house. The craziest part about all of that, is that it actually lessened the pain! Although the pain was excruciating, I was at the point where I could do bits of research to figure out what was wrong with me. This is where I had figured out about Electromagnetic Frequencies and their effect on the human body. My symptoms were so similar to someone suffering from Electromagnetic

Hypersensitivity that I felt some relief when I thought I had figured it out. The relief was short lived due to the "inconclusive evidence" behind EMFs and their effects.

Other Books by the Author

EHS Warrior: Beating Mold Illness, Lyme Disease, and Electromagnetic Hypersensitivity

Living with one chronic disease is difficult, let alone three. Within this book, the author discusses the journey taken to discover that he had Mold Illness, Lyme Disease, and Electromagnetic Hypersensitivity(EHS). After discovering that he had three chronic diseases, the author discusses all of the symptoms experienced, treatments attempted to cure the diseases, and a step-by-step guide detailing what he would do now if just now diagnosed. If you are looking for a book that discusses what it's like living with a chronic disease, how the diseases were cured, and what everyday life is like afterwards, then look no further.

Children's book: Why Wont Peter Come Out and Play?

Cell phones are addicting, at what age should we allow our children to take part in this addiction? The average age for owning a cell phone is now 10 years old. Is that something that you are okay with as a parent? Or would you rather see your child running around and playing outside? I know my answer, but it's up to you to decide if your child will stay inside on the phone all day or go outside and play.

This book is designed for children of all ages and encourages them to choose a childhood free of the distractions a cell phone may impose. Will Peter come out and play? Or will he sit inside on his phone all day? Read this book and find out today!

Cell Phone Free Pregnancy: Give up your "smart" devices for a smarter pregnancy

Did you know that your cell phone emits radio frequency radiation that is twice as dangerous to an infant than an adult? Or that the radiation emitted from your wifi router can cause learning disabilities in your child? Join the movement sweeping the nation of mothers-to-be putting down their cell phones, turning off their wifi routers, and getting rid of their "smart" devices. The goal is a healthier pregnancy, the results are much more than that. In this book you will learn why a cell phone free pregnancy is a smarter pregnancy, as well as tips and tricks on how to eliminate harmful radiation from your life. The science is there and the results are clear, cell phones are <u>out</u> and healthy pregnancies are <u>in.</u>

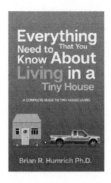

Everything That You Need to Know About Living in a Tiny House: A Complete Guide to Tiny House Living

Find out if the tiny house lifestyle is for you in this captivating book about all of the ins and outs people won't tell you about tiny house living. Learn about everything from securing a mortgage, to what it's like having zero privacy, and even how to change a flat tire. If you are considering tiny house living and don't know where to start, start here.

Acknowledgments

If it weren't for my amazing fiancé, I wouldn't have been healthy enough to write this guide. She truly is an amazing woman and I am eternally grateful for all that she has done for me. I love you, B.

Max and Sam, thank you for letting me stay with you and for allowing me to EMF proof your home. You are amongst the best people I have ever met in my life. No wonder your daughter turned out so remarkable.

Contact the Author

Being that I live a zero EMF lifestyle, contacting me can be accomplished through email only. I personally do not own a cell phone, and never will. If you wish to contact me with any questions, my email is listed below.

Email: Brian@EHSwarrior.com

Website: EHSwarrior.com